50 AMAZING THINGS
You Must See and Do in the Greater D.C. Area

The Ultimate Outdoor Adventure Guide

D1368135

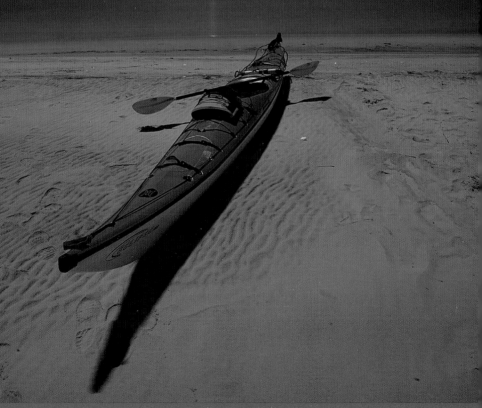

IAN PLANT & JOSEPH ROSSBACH

50 AMAZING THINGS
You Must See and Do in the Greater D.C. Area

The Ultimate Outdoor Adventure Guide

IAN PLANT & JOSEPH ROSSBACH

MOUNTAIN TRAIL

PRESS

Celebrating America's Most Scenic Places

www.mountaintrailpress.com

Book design: Ian Plant
Copy editor: Abbey Greer
Entire Contents Copyright © 2009 Mountain Trail Press
Photographs and text © Ian Plant and Joseph Rossbach
All Rights Reserved
No part of this book may be reproduced in any
form without written permission from the publisher.
Published by Mountain Trail Press
1818 Presswood Road
Johnson City, TN 37604
ISBN: 978-0-9799171-9-6
Printed in China
First Printing, Spring 2009

Library of Congress Control Number: 2009900506

Front cover: Hiking atop North Fork Mountain, West Virginia (self portrait by Joseph Rossbach).

Title page: Kayak camping on the Chesapeake Bay, Maryland (by Ian Plant).

Previous pages: Snow geese migration at Bombay Hook National Wildlife Refuge, Delaware (by Ian Plant).

Left: Autumn color atop Dolly Sods, West Virginia (by Joseph Rossbach).

CLOSE TO HOME

1 Great Falls
2 Huntley Meadows
3 Ghost Fleet of the Potomac
4 Bull Run Spring
5 Kilgore Falls
6 Appalachian Spring
7 Chimney Rocks
8 Old Rag
9 Whiteoak Canyon
10 Whitetail Deer Fawns
11 Big Falls
12 Calvert Cliffs
13 Potomac Whitewater
14 Annapolis Rocks
15 A Paddle For All Seasons

FARTHER AFIELD

16 Big Schloss
17 Cranesville Swamp
18 Lotus Bloom
19 New Point Comfort
20 Morris Creek
21 Smith Island
22 Janes Island
23 Snow Geese Explosion
24 Assateague Island
25 Big Dunes
26 Horseshoe Crab Spawn
27 Paddle with the Dolphins
28 A Trip Back in Time
29 Trough Creek Canyon
30 Pony Swim
31 Wildflowers and Rock Art
32 Lostland Run Loop
33 Swallow Falls
34 Blackwater Canyon
35 North Fork Mountain
36 Seneca Rocks
37 Bear Rocks
38 Rohrbaugh Plains
39 Crabtree Falls
40 Blue Ridge Traverse
41 Sharp Top
42 Paw Paw Tunnel
43 McAfee Knob
44 Devil's Marbleyard
45 Beartown Rocks
46 High Falls of the Cheat

EPIC ADVENTURES

47 Appalachian Trail Traverse
48 Bike Skyline Drive
49 Potomac Adventure
50 Virginia Coast Reserve

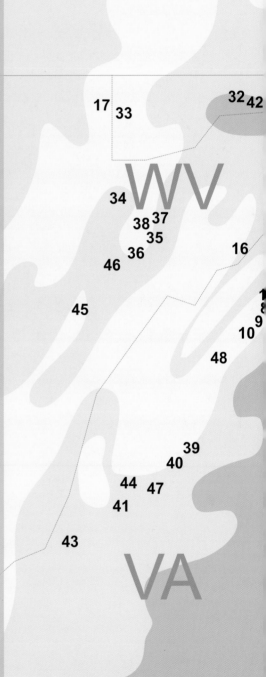

Table of Contents

Close to Home

1   Great Falls   18
2   Huntley Meadows   22
3   Ghost Fleet of the Potomac   24
4   Bull Run Spring   26
5   Kilgore Falls   28
6   Appalachian Spring   30
7   Chimney Rocks   32
8   Old Rag   34
9   Whiteoak Canyon   38
10 Whitetail Deer Fawns   40
11 Big Falls   42
12 Calvert Cliffs   44
13 Potomac Whitewater   46
14 Annapolis Rocks   48
15 A Paddle For All Seasons   50

Farther Afield

16 Big Schloss   54
17 Cranesville Swamp   56
18 Lotus Bloom   58
19 New Point Comfort   60
20 Morris Creek   62
21 Smith Island   64
22 Janes Island   68
23 Snow Geese Explosion   70
24 Assateague Island   72
25 Big Dunes   76
26 Horseshoe Crab Spawn   78
27 Paddle with the Dolphins   80
28 A Trip Back in Time   82
29 Trough Creek Canyon   86
30 Pony Swim   88
31 Wildflowers and Rock Art   90
32 Lostland Run Loop   92
33 Swallow Falls   94
34 Blackwater Canyon   96
35 North Fork Mountain   100
36 Seneca Rocks   104
37 Bear Rocks   106
38 Rohrbaugh Plains   108
39 Crabtree Falls   112
40 Blue Ridge Traverse   114
41 Sharp Top   116
42 Paw Paw Tunnel   118
43 McAfee Knob   120
44 Devil's Marbleyard   122
45 Beartown Rocks   124
46 High Falls of the Cheat   126

Epic Adventures

47 Appalachian Trail Traverse   130
48 Bike Skyline Drive   132
49 Potomac Adventure   136
50 Virginia Coast Reserve   138

Dedications

To my wife Kristin, and our two cats Kali and Stinky Pete, for putting up with my absence as I worked on this book.

—Ian Plant

To my wife Amber and my son Phoenix, for their love and support.

—Joseph Rossbach

Introduction

Those of you living in the greater Washington, D.C. area are incredibly lucky, though you may not realize it. With mind-numbing urban sprawl, gridlocked traffic, and a population approaching 20 million, it sometimes seems that nature is very far away. But that is not so. In fact, as it turns out, you're pretty close to some of the most incredible natural areas and wildlife events on the planet. That is, if you can make it to these places through all that traffic...

We are professional nature photographers, so it is our job to go forth and seek amazing things to photograph. We've both been living within and exploring the area for years; we dare say we know some spots like the backs of our hands. We've traveled by car, foot, bike, canoe, and kayak, logging thousands of miles in our search for the incredible and sublime. As such, we're uniquely qualified to offer up some exceptional outdoor adventures.

This book seeks to identify all of the best scenery, hikes, paddles, and seasonal and wildlife events within a three to four hour's drive of the greater D.C. area. Northern Virginia, Maryland, West Virginia, southern Pennsylvania, and Delaware all fall within the book's range, giving you plenty of opportunities to explore.

With this book, you will unlock the region's secrets. You can witness the massive Delaware Bay horseshoe crab spawn by the full moon, stand in a hidden wildflower glen, or put yourself to the test of Shenandoah's Old Rag Mountain—a rite of passage for the local hiking elite. Or see and do many other amazing things; there are so many to choose!

This book is for anyone who fancies themself an outdoor adventurer, wildlife lover, or overall nature fanatic. We've tried to present a healthy mix of easy, moderate, and downright epic adventures. Many of the things described in this book may challenge mind, body, and spirit; others will give you the chance to explore, wander, and soak in the glory of nature.

So fight the rush hour traffic and get out there. Some amazing things await—50, to be precise!

Trail along North Fork Mountain in West Virginia (Joseph Rossbach).

A wild pony on Assateague Island (Ian Plant).

What this book is . . . and isn't.

One *could* make the argument that this book is really a guide book for nature photographers, masquerading as a guide book for the general public. Although we won't specifically deny these charges, we would like to point out that we did in fact try to write this book for everyone, whether you have ever picked up a camera or not. That said, nature photographers may find this book especially helpful, and the rest of you should definitely consider bringing a camera along when you attempt the amazing things described in this book! We've included helpful photo tips where there was space to cram them in, something that both photographers and casual point-and-shooters alike might find useful.

This book is NOT like your typical guidebook. It does not have turn-by-turn directions that guide you along the path. Most guide books have more detail than you can possibly use: "at 3.2 miles, the trail veers slightly left past an old stump that was once sat on by somebody you've never heard of . . ." You get the idea. We decided instead to keep our descriptions short, with no more information than you need to find your way. We have tried to keep this book small, light, and easily portable, another thing than cannot be said of many guidebooks.

Our maps and trail, paddle, and biking descriptions are meant for general orientation purposes only, and don't describe or show every road, little stream, or side path that you might encounter. They should be enough to get you where you are going, but use your own common sense; trail conditions change over time, natural features appear and disappear as a result of weather or other events, and park managers sometimes decide to close access to certain areas for various good and sundry reasons. All of these things can render our descriptions or maps quickly and suddenly obsolete. So it might be wise to bring current USGS maps or NOAA charts along with you as a precaution—these are made by folks who make maps for a living, and have all sorts of detailed (and usually correct) information that may be useful in case you accidently wander off the path.

In some cases there are simply too many things to do in any given area. Where appropriate, we have included "nearby attractions" to other local hot spots. And sometimes we just let you know that the area has more to offer; additional research on your part may be required in order for you to fully and safely explore these options. We encourage you to do so; there simply is so much that the area has to offer, it was difficult for us to limit this book to only 50 things. Perhaps we'll need to come out with a sequel sometime soon!

This book seeks to inspire you to head out and experience some truly amazing things. We hope that you will view these as life-altering events—they have been for us. We also hope that you actually accomplish all of the 50 amazing things we list here. To that end, we have included a handy checklist at the back of the book so that you can keep track of all of your adventures! Just remember that it's the journey, not the destination, that's the most important thing—so above all, enjoy yourself!

Before you venture out . . .

Basic Gear

No matter what type of activity you do, some basic gear will help keep you safe, warm, and dry. Raingear and extra layers of synthetic clothing (such as fleece) come in handy when the weather turns bad. Water treatment (either a filter or chemical treatment) is recommended for anytime you collect fresh water for drinking. A compass, GPS, and up-to-date topographical maps or nautical charts are highly recommended. Always bring a first aid kit, as well as a whistle or other signaling device, just in case something bad happens. Remember that cell phones don't always have coverage, especially in the kind of out-of-the-way places featured in this book. Bring a flashlight and spare batteries in case you get caught in the field after dark, as well as waterproof matches should you be forced to stop for the night. Sunscreen and a wide-brimmed hat come in handy whenever the sun is out.

Let Someone Know Where You Are

Before departing for a trip, leave a detailed itinerary with a friend or relative. Include where you are going, the phone numbers and names of anyone going with you, where you plan on leaving a vehicle, your expected route, and when you plan to return from your trip.

Hiking

Although relatively safe compared to many outdoor activities, hiking nonetheless can present several dangers. Paths—mountain paths in particular—can at times be steep, rocky, and/or slick, and hikers risk twisting an ankle, falling, or worse. Trails are not always clearly marked; navigation skills and some common sense come in handy. Make sure that you have proper skills and proper gear before hitting the trail. Waterproof hiking boots help protect ankles from twisting and help keep your feet dry in wet and muddy conditions. Several poisonous snakes live in the region, including copperhead, cottonmouth, and timber rattlesnake—so keep an eye out.

Paddling

Being on the water presents a unique set of challenges and dangers. Water can hurt you two ways: drowning and exposure. To prevent the first, always wear a personal flotation device (PFD) when on the water. To prevent the second, wear a wetsuit in cold weather, and a drysuit in really cold weather. Remember, even on a warm day, long-term exposure to water can cause hyperthermia, so be prepared for the worst that could happen. Consider taking a course to learn basic paddling and rescue skills. Be especially aware of incoming bad weather; get back to shore if it looks like a storm is coming and seek shelter. If caught in a lighting storm while in an open marsh, sit on top of your PFD and stay as low to the ground as possible. If paddling on the Chesapeake or its tidal waterways, note that much of the terrain is a maze of salt marsh, with countless channels and meandering waterways. It is easy to get lost if you don't keep your wits about you. A spare paddle, as well as a paddle float and bilge pump—and knowing how to use them—are useful in case you capsize. For those who are less comfortable with their paddling ability, avoid trips to open water areas that may be subject to wind, waves, and strong tidal currents.

Biking

Make sure you carry basic repair equipment with you, including tire patch kits and a spare tire tube or two. Always wear a helmet. Be polite to others using the trail.

Leave No Trace

Simply put, Leave No Trace ethics require that you leave a place in its natural state. Carry out all of your trash (if you see other people's trash, you should grab that as well). For human waste, dig a "cat hole" that is at least eight inches deep and cover it when finished; in ecologically sensitive areas, pack human waste out with you. Clean up your campsite when done, and try to make it look like you were never there. Avoid disturbing or harassing animals, especially when they are nesting.

Cascades on Lostland Run (Joseph Rossbach).

LOCAL EXCURSIONS

Great Falls of the Potomac (Ian Plant).

Great Falls
Great Falls Park, Virginia & C&O Canal National Historic Park, Maryland

Highlights: *Huge waterfalls, raging rapids, a scenic gorge, and great wildlife and outdoor sports watching opportunities.*

Few words can describe the power and splendor of Great Falls of the Potomac. Straddling the Virginia and Maryland border, this scenic wonder occurs where the Potomac crosses the "fall line" separating the piedmont from the coastal plain. Here, the river plunges over seventy feet in a quarter-mile through raging rapids, and then winds its way through towering 100-foot cliffs for several miles. It's a sight not to be missed.

Great blue heron (Ian Plant).

Not only is the scenery superlative, but the wildlife is pretty impressive as well. Great blue herons frequent the falls during the summer, daring the raging waters to hunt for fish. It's a real thrill to watch one of these graceful and seemingly delicate birds suddenly plunge into the thundering rapids and emerge unscathed, prize firmly within its grasp.

The outdoor activities here are boundless; in fact, viewing one of the most popular activities is a big draw in itself. You're almost always guaranteed to see daredevil whitewater kayakers at Great Falls, surfing in the rapids below the big drops. Sometimes, if you are lucky, you can see kayakers going over the falls in a thrilling and dramatic free-fall! In addition to

kayaking, the cliffs of Mather Gorge, just below the falls, attract hundreds of gravity-defying rock climbers.

For the less hardcore adventurer, hiking and biking trails abound on both the Virginia and Maryland sides of the river, and short jaunts take you to scenic overlooks above the falls. On the Maryland side, bicyclists can enjoy the many scenic miles of the **Chesapeake & Ohio Canal Towpath**. A very popular hiking trail is the **Billy Goat Trail**, which follows a strenuous route through the steep cliffs along Mather Gorge. To reach the Billy Goat Trail, follow the towpath south from the parking area until you see signs for the trail; take a right and begin a scenic scramble over boulders and up steep rock faces (not too steep, mind you). The Billy Goat Trail ends at the towpath; go left to return to the parking lot.

On the Virginia side, there's another great circuit hike. Take the **River Trail** to the **Ridge Trail**, both of which follow along the edge of Mather Gorge. Along the way you'll pass the historic ruins of the old Patowmack Canal (built by a company owned by George Washington). The Ridge Trail ends at the **Difficult Run Trail**; take a right to travel along a beautiful

Activities: Hiking, biking, kayaking, rock climbing, wildlife watching.

Access Points: Great Falls Park (VA side); Chesapeake & Ohio Canal National Historic Park (MD side).

Entrance fees: $5/vehicle VA side; $4/vehicle MD side.

Best time of year: Any.

An expert kayaker runs Great Falls (Ian Plant).

stream with cascading waterfalls. When you reach the trailhead parking area for the Difficult Run trail, cross Georgetown Pike and take an informal trail for about a quarter mile or so, and take a right when you hit a large dirt road, which is actually the Ridge Trail again. Hike a short distance and take your first left on the **Old Carriage Road** back to the Great Falls visitor center. The many old carriage roads in this area are also very popular with mountain bikers.

Total hiking distance: *MD side 3 miles round trip; VA side 5 miles round trip.*

Total hiking time: *MD side 1-2 hours; VA side 2-3 hours.*

Elevation gain: *Little elevation gain but a fair amount of scrambling over rocks and boulders.*

Directions to trailhead: *To reach the Maryland side, exit the Capital Beltway (Route 495) at the Clara Barton Parkway. Head west on the parkway until reaching MacArthur Boulevard, and*
turn left. Take MacArthur Boulevard into the Chesapeake & Ohio Canal National Historic Park. To reach the Virginia side, exit the Beltway at the Great Falls/ Langley Exit. Turn left on Georgetown Pike. Proceed approximately six miles before turning right at a stop light onto Old Dominion Drive to enter Great Falls Park. Park near the visitor center.

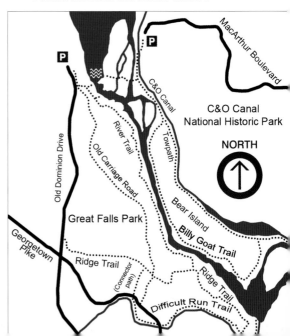

Photo Tips: Although the park overlooks offer stunning views, the best photo opportunities can be found when you get closer to the water's edge. Fisherman's Eddy on the Virginia side is a steep access point used by kayakers and fishermen (as the name implies). Use care when scrambling over the slick and sometimes wet boulders. Both sunrise and sunset are good times to photograph Great Falls and Mather Gorge.

Sunrise over Great Falls of the Potomac (Joseph Rossbach)

Huntley Meadows
Huntley Meadows Park, Virginia

Highlights: *A short hike to a beautiful freshwater marsh that is home to various species of birds, right in the middle of the greater D.C. metro area.*

A wild oasis in the heart of an urban desert, Huntley Meadows lies in a wet lowland that was carved out by an ancient meander of the Potomac River. Although located in the middle of Alexandria, you'd never know that you were in one of the most densely populated suburbs of the sprawl-ing D.C. Metro area. And luckily, the birds don't know it either. Huntley Meadows attracts a great variety of bird species throughout the year, including bald eagles, kingfishers, great blue herons, great and snowy egrets, green herons, Virginia rails, bitterns, red-winged blackbirds, Canada geese . . . oh, you get the idea, the list goes on and on! Chances are you'll spot some non-bird species as well, including deer, beaver, and snapping turtles. Most species seem to be more active in the early morning or late evening.

From the parking area, head down the wide graded trail leading to the meadows through an open forest. When you get to your first fork in the trail, stay right on the

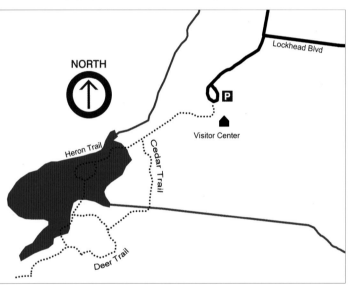

Heron Trail. The Heron Trail soon enters the meadows and becomes a boardwalk. Although you may hear the sound of traffic in the background, it is muffled by the more present sound of songbirds and honking geese. Soon you are immersed in a wetland environment, surrounded on all sides by water, marsh grass, and animal activity.

As you proceed, the boardwalk becomes trail again, passes an observation tower, and then becomes boardwalk again. The tower is a great place to stop and look for birds from up high. After the tower, take a left on the **Deer Trail**. The trails are not always well marked, except for the occasional "you are here" sign. In a short distance you will take a right on the **Cedar Trail**, which will lead you to the intersection with the Heron Trail and back to the parking area. There are a number of other informal trails heading off in all directions; feel free to explore more of the park to your heart's content.

Total hiking distance: *2-3 miles round trip.*

Total hiking time: *1-2 hours.*

Elevation gain: *None.*

Directions to trailhead: *The parking area for Huntley Meadows is located off of Lockhead Boulevard, which can be reached from Route 1 in the Hybla Valley area of Alexandria.*

A heron hunts in the marshes of Huntley Meadows (Ian Plant).

Activities: Hiking, bird watching.

Access Points: Alexandria, Virginia.

Entrance fees: None.

Best time of year: Any.

Ghost Fleet of the Potomac
Potomac River, Maryland

Highlights: *A scenic paddle along the Potomac River to a ship's graveyard.*

During World War I, Congress embarked on an ambitious ship-building program to help put the nation on a war footing. As part of this effort, it authorized the construction of several hundred wooden-hulled transport ships. Political infighting, excessive bureaucratic red tape, and various technical problems delayed construction of the ships, so that when the war ended, not a single one of the wooden boats had set sail across the Atlantic. When world trade contracted after the war, the ships were rendered useless. After laying idle for decades, they eventually were abandoned in little known Mallows Bay, a shallow out-of-the-way bay on the tidal Potomac River.

Mallows Bay is home to about 150 abandoned ships, making it one of the largest ship's graveyards in the world. Over time, the forgotten ships have mostly rotted away, but a few ships still poke above the waterline. Satellite pictures of the area

Looking out at Mallows Bay from the rusted hulk of the "Accomac" (Ian Plant).

show the outlines of dozens of ship hulls below the waterline. The ships now provide habitat for fish and birds, and make an excellent place to spend the day exploring by canoe or kayak!

The closest access point to Mallows Bay is Purse State Park, which unfortunately does not have a formal boat launch area or auto access directly to the water. A short carry across the road and then down a trail for about a quarter of a mile from the parking area is necessary to reach the water. Purse State Park's sandy beach makes an excellent launching place, and also a great place to explore on foot. Fossil gathering is a favorite activity of many of the park's visitors, with shark's teeth being the most common fossils found.

Heading upriver (north) from the park, you will paddle for about 2.5 miles to reach Mallows Bay. Kayaks are ideal for this trip; although canoes will be fine in calm weather. The Potomac River is wide here, and can get rough in high winds. Mallows Bay is the second bay you encounter on the trip, and is easily identified by the presence of a giant rusted iron shipwreck, an abandoned old ferry called the "Accomac."

Although most of the ships have rotted below the waterline, a few, including the Accomac, still have material above the water. Some of the ships have collected sediment and have become "islands" supporting plant growth. Use caution if you decide to land on any of the ships, as rusted metal and rotten timbers may break easily. The remains of the ships themselves

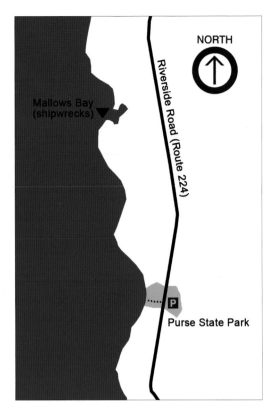

create quite a navigation hazard; rusted iron spikes and old wood stick out of the water, or worse, are just below the water line. So please be careful and keep an eye out for potential hazards.

Total paddling distance: *About five miles round trip.*

Total paddling time: *3-4 hours.*

Paddling conditions: *Tidal flatwater; can get choppy in rough weather.*

Directions to boat launch: *From the Capital Beltway (Route 495), take Route 210 (Indian Head Highway) south for 18.8 miles. Turn left onto Hawthorne Road, and then after 0.4 miles take a right onto Chicamuxen Road. After 8.5 miles, turn right onto Riverside Road, which takes you 6.7 miles to Purse State Park. The parking area is on the left, less than two miles after you pass the intersection with Liverpool Road.*

Activities: Kayaking, canoeing.

Access Points: Indian Head, Maryland.

Entrance fees: No.

Best times of year: Spring through autumn.

Bull Run Spring
Bull Run Regional Park, Virginia

Highlights: *Wildflowers, wildflowers, wildflowers galore as you hike along a scenic stream. Did we mention the wildflowers?*

The Bull Run-Occoquan Trail stretches 18 miles between Bull Run Regional Park and Fountainhead Regional Park. A scenic hike worthy of attention anytime of year, something truly magical happens every spring: wildflowers bloom in a profusion unrivaled by almost anything else in the Mid-Atlantic area. Their rival can only be found in two other places—Thompson Wildlife Management Area in Virginia and Shenk's Ferry Wildflower Preserve in Pennsylvania—both conveniently described elsewhere in this book, of course! Come mid-April, the loamy flood plain surrounding the famous Bull Run is carpeted with acres and acres of bluebells and spring beauties, as well as other species including trout lily, Dutchman's breeches, and many more.

The northern terminus of the trail is at Bull Run Regional Park, which showcases the most impressive display of Virginia bluebells anywhere in the state. To commemorate the event, the park has set up a short loop trail called—well, you guessed it—the **Bluebell Trail**, so that visitors may enjoy the experience.

Upon entering the park, follow signs to parking for the Bluebell Trail. The two ends of the trail loop don't quite meet up, so you'll have to walk a short distance on the park road to connect the two. Taking the northernmost end of the loop (the one closest to the parking area), you begin your hike through open forest. This trail can be very muddy in the spring—it is, after all, a flood plain! So bring appropriate waterproof footgear.

Soon you reach Cub Run, where the trail turns south following the course of its meanders. Here's where the action starts. Bluebells and spring beauties literally carpet the forest floor around the banks of

Bluebells carpet the forest floor in April (Ian Plant).

Flowers carpet the Bull Run flood plain (Ian Plant).

the sluggish river. You'll see nothing but flowers for the rest of the hike.

Soon the trail meets up with Bull Run. A path comes in from the left, crossing Bull Run. This is the Bull Run-Occoquan Trail, so unless you want to hike 18 miles, do not take this trail! Instead, continue to the right on the Bluebell Trail, now following the course of Bull Run until you exit back to the park road, just a short jaunt from where you parked your car.

If you are feeling more adventurous, plan a hike along the Bull Run-Occoquan Trail. You'll find bluebells in profusion in certain areas along the trail, and a change of scenery here and there as Bull Run varies between flat water and white water in places. The trail passes through three other parks, allowing you to choose different mileage options: Hemlock Overlook Regional Park, Bull Run Marina, and Fountainhead Regional Park, which is the trail's southern terminus. You will need to leave a shuttle car at one of these destinations.

Please note that any hike along Cub or Bull Run is along a flood plain. Heavy rains can cause the water to rise very fast and flood the trail, turning a pleasant hike into a wet slog, covering the bluebells in unpleasant mud, and turning small stream crossings into a challenge.

Total hiking distance: *1.5 miles round trip.*

Total hiking time: *1-2 hours.*

Elevation gain: *None.*

Directions to trailhead: *Take Route 66 to Exit 52 (Route 29) at Centreville, drive 2 miles south, turn left onto Bull Run Post Office Road and follow the signs to the park entrance.*

Activities: Hiking.

Access Points: Manassas, Virginia.

Entrance fees: Free for residents of Alexandria, Arlington, City of Fairfax, Fairfax County, Falls Church and Loudoun; $7 for everyone else.

Best times of year: Mid to late April.

5 Kilgore Falls
Rocks State Park, Maryland

Highlights: *A short and pleasant hike to one of Maryland's prettiest—and least visited—waterfalls.*

Activities: Hiking.

Access Points: Bel Air, Maryland.

Entrance fees: None.

Best times of year: Anytime.

Rocks State Park is a little known gem resting in Harford County, Maryland, close to the Pennsylvania border. In 1993, the state acquired privately owned land around Falling Creek, which includes a little known and Maryland's second highest free falling waterfall, Kilgore Falls (other falls in Maryland may be higher, but are cascading falls rather than free falling). Also known as Falling Creek Falls or Falling Branch Falls, Kilgore Falls is an easy hike with great rewards. Falling Branch passes swiftly through a deep gorge known as Kilgore Rocks, from which Kilgore Falls drops over erosion-resistant schist into a plunge pool below.

Pick up the trail just off of Falling Branch Road and walk into the lush woodlands, crossing a footbridge in a short distance from the parking lot. Although this is a short hike, the scenery and woodlands are absolutely beautiful. Thick moss-covered rocks and ferns line the trail as you approach closer to Falling Branch. Before you reach the river, a path will head right. If you wish to check it out, this path takes you to the top of the falls for a scenic view down into the gorge (the path is not worth taking past the falls, as it soon ends at a cornfield and power line right of way).

Continuing on the main path, ford Falling Branch via a series of stone steps and turn right (there will be another trail that

Below Kilgore Falls (Ian Plant).

Kilgore Falls in autumn (Joseph Rossbach).

Nearby attractions: If hiking to the Falls doesn't satisfy your appetite for adventure, consider a trip to the main portion of Rocks State Park. There, you can take a short hike to the top of the King and Queen Seat, a massive rock outcropping 190 feet high rising above the park with majestic views of the surrounding woods and farmland. The King and Queens Seat is believed to be an ancient ceremonial site of the Susquehanna Indians, and once you reach its towering summit high above Deer Creek, it's easy to understand why they may have used this place to conduct rituals and give thanks to the gods.

heads left which may be worth exploring later if you wish to stretch your legs a bit more, but otherwise it is unremarkable). Kilgore Falls is now in sight, and its tumbling waters momentarily deafen the sound of song birds and wind pulsing through the forest canopy above.

Kilgore Falls plunges 17 feet over a short cliff. Although not very high, the interesting geology of the cliff makes this a beautiful place. In the summer, a quick dip in the frigid waters of the deep plunge pool below the falls will cool you off and reinvigorate your senses. When you are done soaking in the subtle beauty of the falls, head back the way you came.

Total hiking distance: 1.1 miles round trip.

Total hiking time: 1-2 hours.

Elevation gain: Minimal.

Directions to trailhead: From Route 95 north of Baltimore, take exit 77B. Follow Route 24 north through the towns of Bel Air and Forest Hill. After 13.4 miles on Route 24 you will pass the entrance to Rocks State Park on the left; continue on Route 24 for another 4.2 miles and turn left onto St. Mary's Road. Go another 0.4 miles and turn right onto Falling Branch Road; park in the small dirt parking area on the right (the sign is marked as "Rocks State Park, Falling Branch Area").

6

Appalachian Spring
Thompson Wildlife Management Area, Virginia

Highlights: One of the best large-flowered trillium displays in the country, and a trip along the magnificent Appalachian Trail.

Large flowered trillium (Ian Plant).

Every spring, something magical happens on the upland slopes of the Thompson Wildlife Management Area in Virginia. For a short period of time, hundreds of thousands of large-flowered trillium blooms literally carpet the forest floor for as far as the eye can see. It is an amazing event (hence its inclusion in this book), but if you blink you might miss it. The trillium only bloom for a short period of time between the end of April and the beginning of May. So don't procrastinate!

As you take Freezeland Road up to the top of the mountain crest, you'll quickly figure out when you've gotten to the right spot;

trillium will start to line the roadway everywhere. There are a number of parking areas along the road, all of which make good places to get out and explore. The most popular is the Trillium Parking Area, which puts you in the heart of the spring trillium explosion.

From the parking area it is a short walk to the famous Appalachian Trail. Turn left, turn right, it doesn't matter; either way you can travel for several miles before the trillium runs out. We don't propose a specific hike for this entry; just wander to your heart's content. Be careful if leaving the trail, as the trillium blooms are very delicate and easy to trample underfoot.

Both there-and-back or shuttle hikes are possible here. The trails are fairly easy, without too much up or down, unless you go far enough along the Appalachian Trail to leave the mountain crest. Just remember that it is over a thousand miles either north or south before you hit either end of the Trail!

Trillium won't be the only flowers you see. There are plenty of other species that grow in abundance here, including mayapple, orchids, violets, wild geranium, star chickweed, and rue anemone, among others. Wildlife also lives in abundance in the area; if you are lucky you might see deer, turkey, racoon, woodcock, or grouse.

Activities: Hiking, backpacking.

Access Points: Linden, Virginia.

Entrance fees: None.

Best times of year: Late April through early May.

Appalachian Trail (Ian Plant).

Total hiking distance: *1-3 miles.*

Total hiking time: *1-2 hours.*

Elevation gain: *Minimal.*

Directions to trailhead: *From Route 66 take Exit 18 (VA-688) toward Markham. Take a left on to Leeds Manor Road (VA-168). Turn right onto John Marshall Highway (VA-55). Drive four*

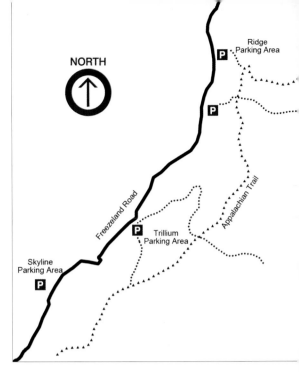

miles on VA-55, taking a right onto Freezeland Road. Drive up to the top of the mountain, and look for the various parking areas on both sides of the road. The Trillium Parking Area is right before you reach a radio tower.

Large flowered trillium (Ian Plant).

7

Chimney Rocks
Catoctin Mountain Park, Maryland

Highlights: *A hike past one of Maryland's prettiest waterfalls to several scenic overlooks with unusual geology.*

Nestled in the Appalachian Mountains of west central Maryland is a wonderful place knows as Catoctin Mountain Park. Managed by the National Park Service, this area of pristine hardwood forests, wild mountain streams, abundant mountain laurel and rocky vistas lies just 50 miles north of Washington, D.C. The park is arguably best known for its neighbors, Camp David—the presidential retreat—and Cunningham Falls State Park, home to a 78-foot cascading waterfall. While Camp David is obviously off limits, this hike loops through the best that Catoctin has to offer, with a side trip to see Cunningham Falls.

From the Visitor Center, take the **Falls Nature Trail**, which heads toward Cunningham Falls and the trail to Hog Rock. When you reach the intersection with the trail to Hog Rock (all trail intersections are marked with signposts), turn left and descend to Route 77. Crossing the road, you make a brief foray into Cunningham Falls State Park, taking a short boardwalk path to the base of Cunningham Falls.

After visiting the falls, backtrack, cross Route 77 again, and take the trail up toward Hog Rock. The trail takes you through a beautiful section of hardwood forest, which will be ablaze with vivid autumn color come October and November. The trail is bordered with dogwood trees, which in late spring and early summer put on a lovely display of white flowers.

Hog Rock is the first of several vistas you will pass. After Hog Rock, continue past an intersection with the Park Central Road and head to Blue Ridge Summit Overlook. Next head toward Thurmont Vista, with a view of its namesake town in the valley below. After Thurmont Vista, your next stop is Wolf Rock. Wolf Rock is named for its resemblance to the snout and head of a wolf (okay, so you may have to use your imagination on this one). Wolf Rock not only has a great view, but some interesting geology as well.

Continue past Wolf Rock towards Chimney Rock. Chimney Rock is reached by a spur trail on your right. From the rocky outcrop, you can see Cat Rock standing at 1,500 feet visible to the southeast, and the mountains and hills of the Catoctin rage fall off into the distance. The view is breathtaking, and you should spend some time just sitting and enjoying the vista.

Back on the trail, continue heading around the loop until you reach an intersection with the trail heading toward Wolf Rock. Turn left, and then turn left again to head back to the visitor center.

Total hiking distance: *7 mile loop.*

Total hiking time: *4-5 hours.*

Elevation gain: *700 feet with a lot of up and down.*

Directions to trailhead: *Head north on Route 270 for 32 miles and exit on to Route 15 north towards Fredrick/ Thurmont. Go 17 miles on Route 15 and exit on to Route 77 at Thurmont. Travel 3.0 miles to the Catoctin Mountain Park visitor center on the right.*

Activities: Hiking.

Access Points: Thurmont, Maryland.

Entrance fees: None.

Best times of year: April through October.

Chimney Rock in winter (Ian Plant).

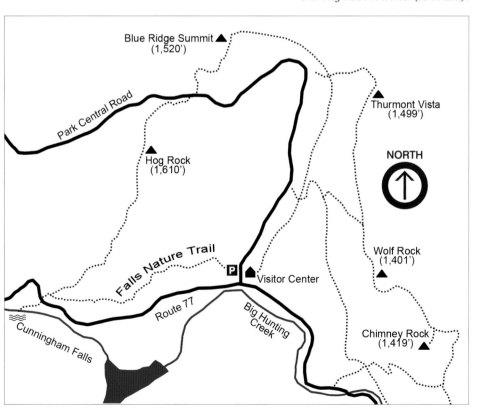

Old Rag Mountain
Shenandoah National Park, Virginia

Highlights: *A challenging hike and rock scramble though a maze of boulders, chasms, and caves. Incredible 360-degree views from the summit.*

Old Rag Mountain in Shenandoah National Park is the best hike in the greater D.C. area; in fact, Old Rag Mountain is one of the best hikes in the country. It is simply that good. With great views, incredible geology, and a trail that leads through a maze of boulders, chasms, and caves, it is no wonder that Old Rag draws huge crowds. So huge, you might literally get caught in a traffic jam on the trail!

Old Rag, both literally and figuratively, stands alone. This 3,291-foot granite outcrop is set apart from the main line of the Blue Ridge Mountains, and it has wonderful 360-degree views of surrounding farmland, rolling piedmont, and the major peaks along Skyline Drive. This spectacular view draws over 100,000 hikers every year, especially during the spring bloom and autumn.

This trail is very difficult and should not be attempted by those who are in poor shape or who have heart problems. Hikers should bring proper footwear (that is, hiking boots), plenty of water (most of the hike is on a high ridge away from any water sources), and cold weather and rain gear appropriate for the season. That said, this hike is a whale of a good time, and the views are worth the effort, so bring plenty of patience and a good attitude!

Starting from the lower parking lot, hike up the road for a little less than a mile to the upper parking lot (if you arrive early, late, off-season, or during the week, you might be able to find parking at the small up-

per lot, but usually it is filled up early in the day). From the upper parking lot, take the blue-blazed **Ridge Trail** to begin your hike up Old Rag. You will steadily climb through a series of gradual switchbacks for about two miles before reaching the long open ridge to the summit. Views get more frequent and better the higher you climb.

Once you reach the open ridge, the fun begins in earnest. Your next mile to the summit is less hiking and more, well, *rock-scrambling* and even *rock-climbing* at times. You pass through a maze of boulders, deep clefts, natural staircases, and even caves, seemingly on your hands and knees as much as you are on your feet. The whole time you are treated with amazing views of the surrounding countryside and the Old Rag summit massif. Caution is needed when hiking this section, as parts can be slippery and steep. The worse thing you are likely to encounter, however, is a traffic jam! Some points on the hike serve as natural bottlenecks for hikers, and you might have to wait a few minutes before you can get through.

Natural staircase (Ian Plant).

After some steep rocky sections, the trail levels somewhat for the last few tenths of a mile until you reach the summit. After a long and exhausting climb, all your weariness will pass when you are treated to the glorious view. The summit resembles a giant's marble-yard, with house-sized boulders leaning precariously against each other or balanced on the edge of a cliff, looking like a simple push will send them

Old Rag's boulder-strewn summit (Ian Plant).

tumbling hundreds of feet below. Hop, scramble, or climb to the tops of the boulders for a wonderful 360-degree panorama view of the Blue Ridge Mountains and surrounding countryside. Geological oddities abound, including dozens of potholes that were probably formed when the cliffs were higher and a stream flowed through this area. Sit back, relax, and enjoy the scenery, if not solitude—you will likely not be alone!

After leaving the summit, continue south

Activities: Hiking, backcountry camping, rock climbing.

Access Points: Sperryville, Virginia.

Entrance fees: $5/adult.

Best times of year: Early summer (June and July), autumn (late October and early November).

along the Ridge Trail. You will descend for about a third of a mile before reaching the Byrd's Nest Shelter, a three-sided stone shelter (no camping is allowed, but it makes a great place to stop for a snack). Turning right on the blue-blazed **Saddle Trail**, you descend for another two-thirds of a mile before passing the Old Rag Shelter (this time a wooden three-sided shelter; once again no camping is allowed). From the Old Rag Shelter the trail widens and follows a forestry road for another half-mile before reaching the intersection of the Berry Hollow Fire Road, Old Rag Fire Road, and Weakley Hollow Fire Road. Turn right downhill on the yellow-blazed **Weakley Hollow Fire Road**. This broad dirt road leads two miles back to the upper parking lot.

Hikers, if lucky, may have the opportunity to spot wildlife including wild turkey, deer, snakes (watch out for rattlesnakes!), and black bear. During the early summer months of June and July, azalea and mountain laurel bloom on Old Rag's steep slopes, painting the landscape in red and

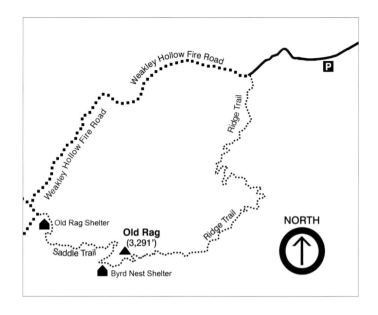

white. Late October through early November is a great time to view autumn's finery. Winter can bring cold temperatures, biting winds, snow, ice, and maybe even solitude, a rare commodity on Old Rag! Crampons and an ice axe might be needed if conditions are particularly bad, although Virginia winters usually are fairly mild, even in the mountains.

There are also rock-climbing opportunities on Old Rag's many cliffs, with over 100 established routes ranging from 5.4 to 5.12 in difficulty. Some of the routes are over 100 feet in length. It is beyond the scope of this book to describe these routes and access to them; check climbing guide

books and websites for more information.

Total hiking distance: *8.7 miles round trip from lower parking lot.*

Total hiking time: *5-6 hours.*

Elevation gain: *2,300 feet.*

Directions to trailhead: *From Sperryville, take Route 522, following it south for .8 mile. Turn right onto Route 231 for 8 miles. Turn right onto Route 601 and follow signs to the parking area, approximately 3 miles from Route 231, just beyond Nethers.*

Photo Tips: Being on Old Rag's summit ridge is like the photographer's equivalent of being a kid in a candy store. House-sized boulders, a maze of chasms and caves, and beautiful views in all directions can overwhelm the senses. Sunset or sunrise are great times to be on the top of Old Rag, when the fantastic boulders are bathed in eerie light. This, of course, poses a bit of a problem—being on the summit at these times means traveling several miles in the dark! A good flashlight or headlamp with spare batteries is a must. A bit of helpful advice: under no circumstances should you try to negotiate the boulder maze of the Ridge Trail in the dark. Rather, descend or ascend the mountain (whether you are aiming to be on top at sunset or sunrise) by the backside Saddle Trail and fire roads.

Old Rag's summit at sunset (Ian Plant).

Whiteoak Canyon
Shenandoah National Park, Virginia

Highlights: *A challenging hike along two scenic creeks past a dozen waterfalls; superlative fall color in late October.*

The best place to see waterfalls in the greater D.C. area is Shenandoah National Park. And the best place to see waterfalls in Shenandoah National Park is Whiteoak Canyon and Cedar Run, two very scenic, parallel streams that, when hiked together, make for an incredibly beautiful day hike.

This trail is difficult and should not be attempted in full by those who are in poor shape or have heart problems. Hikers should bring proper footwear (that is, hiking boots) and cold weather and rain gear appropriate for the season. Shorter excursions along the lower parts of this trail, however, are not as difficult and can be very rewarding.

Although this loop hike can be accessed from Skyline Drive, starting from the lower parking lot has one significant advantage: you get to hike *down* on the second half of the loop. Of course, this means that for the first half you must hike *up*, and quite a bit of up at that—with an elevation gain of over 2,500 feet, this hike is not for couch potatoes. Parts of the trail are steep, rocky, and wet, but certainly well worth the effort.

From the parking lot, take the blue-blazed **Whiteoak Canyon Trail**. The trail is relatively flat for the first mile-and-a-half, until reaching the lowest of the many Whiteoak Canyon waterfalls. At this point, the trail steepens and begins to climb in earnest via several switchbacks. The scenery becomes truly superlative as you pass a total of six major waterfalls, numerous smaller cascades, and several sce-

Lower Whiteoak Falls (Ian Plant).

nic overlooks, the best being at the top of the last waterfall, reached at 2.7 miles. At 86-feet high, this waterfall, known only as Whiteoak Canyon Falls #1, is the second tallest in the Park.

Continuing uphill from the main overlook, you will soon cross Whiteoak Canyon Run at a horse trail (if the water is too high, continue up the right side of the Run and cross a footbridge in 120 yards). After crossing, follow the yellow blazed **Whiteoak Fire Road**. In 1.5 miles the fire road will veer right; stay left on the narrower yellow-blazed **Horse Trail** (marked on a concrete post as "Horse Tr To Big Meadows"). While hiking on the fire road and horse trail, you will be away from both views and water, although you will pass through some pretty forest.

In 0.6 miles the horse trail intersects the blue-blazed **Cedar Run Trail**. Turn left downhill to begin your descent of 2.4 miles through Cedar Run Canyon. Although not as grand as the waterfalls of Whiteoak Canyon, Cedar Run's falls have

Activities: Hiking, backcountry camping.

Access Points: Sperryville, Virginia.

Entrance fees: $5/adult.

Best times of year: May-October.

Waterfall along Cedar Run (Ian Plant).

their own quiet beauty. The trail will seem quieter too, as Cedar Run doesn't get the crowds found on Whiteoak. After passing several small waterfalls and innumerable cascades on the way down, you will eventually reach an intersection with the Whiteoak Canyon Trail. Now here's the sad part: turn right to head back to the parking lot and the end of your journey.

Total hiking distance: *8 miles round trip.*

Total hiking time: *5-6 hours.*

Elevation gain: *2,500 feet.*

Directions to trailhead: *From Sperryville, follow Route 522 south for 0.8 miles. Turn right on to Route 231, following it for 10 miles to Etlan. Turn right on Route 643. Travel 4.5 miles and turn right on Route 600 (Berry Hollow Road). In another 4.7 miles you will reach the parking lot.*

Photo Tips: Waterfalls are often best photographed on cloudy or rainy days. Use a polarizing filter to remove glare from wet rocks and to improve the color of foliage.

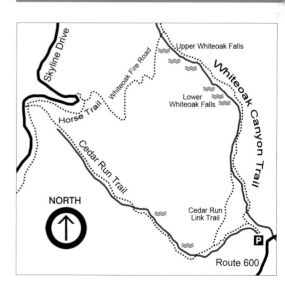

Deer Fawns
Shenandoah National Park, Virginia

Highlights: A hike through an open meadow to see white-tailed deer fawns.

Who doesn't like fawns? Cute and playful, they amuse us with their antics, wobbly legs, and innocent demeaners. There are few symbols of parental devotion more enduring than a mother doe standing watch over her young fawn. If only there was a place where one could go to witness this miracle of nature . . .

Lucky for us, there is! Every June, Shenandoah National Park's Big Meadows area becomes a nursery for dozens of newborn fawns. Not only will you see more deer than you can shake a stick at, it

get's even better: the deer are very habituated to people, allowing you a chance to watch fawns up close and personal. Don't try to get too close and invade the fawns' comfort zone; staying at least thirty feet away seems to be a good rule of thumb. But don't be surprised if a fawn and its mother who become comfortable enough with your presence walk right past you—a thrilling and beautiful gift.

Start your hike at the parking area for the Byrd Visitor Center and wayside station. Cross Skyline Drive (make sure to look both ways for traffic!), and head into the meadows following any one of a number

Nearby attractions: Dark Hollow Falls and Lewis Spring Falls can be found nearby. Dark Hollow Falls is an easy hike from Skyline Drive.

of informal paths. Walk to your heart's content, enjoying the open grasslands, flowers, and ferns. Oh, and don't forget to enjoy the fawns!

The deer are most active in the morning and evening. During the heat of the day they often retreat into the forest for shade and cover. Be careful when walking in deep grass; you don't want to accidentally stumble over a resting fawn.

The fawns are usually born in the first or second week of June. They mature quickly, and by the end of June they usually have gotten quite big, although they retain their white spots for several months to come.

Total hiking distance: 1-2 miles.

Total hiking time: 1-2 hours.

Elevation gain: Negligible.

Directions to trailhead: From the Thornton Gap entrance station, take Skyline Drive south for 20 miles to the Byrd Visitor Center (milepost 51).

Activities: Hiking, wildlife watching.

Access Points: Skyline Drive, Shenandoah National Park, Virginia.

Entrance fees: Up to $15/vehicle; varies depending on time of year.

Best times of year: June.

White-tailed deer fawns (Ian Plant).

Big Falls
Shenandoah National Park, Virginia

Highlights: *A beautiful day hike to Shenandoah's tallest waterfall.*

Shenandoah National Park delivers to the adventurous hiker many of the best trails in the Mid-Atlantic region. One of the best hikes in the park is Big Falls of Overall Run. This waterfall is the highest in the park, dropping 93 feet into a hollow below. From the cliff overlooking the falls, the hiker is rewarded with tremendous views of Big Falls against the backdrop of Page Valley and Massanutten Mountain deep in the distance.

Start the hike by picking up the **Appalachian Trail**. Head south on the AT, entering fern-laden woods and winding along the south flank of Hogback Mountain. Follow the AT until it levels out and intersects with the **Tuscarora Trail** at 0.4 miles; turn right. Finding your way through the woods at the many trail intersections is easily accomplished by referring to the cement posts with clearly marked directions and distances.

Continue following the Tuscarora Trail for another 1.1 miles through a beautiful section of woods along the rocky path until

you reach another trail intersection. Turn right along the **Tuscarora-Overall Run Trail**, and begin your descent down towards the Overall Run watershed. The stair-step fashion of this section of the trail will test your knees and balance as the steep ascent continues. In the spring and fall, the woods are often shrouded in a thick white fog that lends a magical quality of light and atmosphere to the hike.

The trail intersects with the **Mathews Arm Trail** at 2.7 miles. Continue going forward as both trails run together for a short distance before the Mathews Arm trail veers off to the right. The Tuscarora-Overall Run Falls Trail continues heading down, and at 2.9 miles you will reach the first set of falls. At this point, a small side trail leaves the main trail and brings you down to the upper falls of Overall Run. This beautiful set of falls cascades over rock ledges and drops 29 feet. At the base of the falls, a car-sized boulder splits the stream in two; this is a great spot to sit back and enjoy this wild stream. Don't be fooled by the small cascading appearance

Upper Falls of Overall Run (Ian Plant).

of these falls, as Big Falls of Overall Run has yet to come, and at this point you are only a short distance away.

Continue for only another 0.3 miles, following the crest of the canyon, before you reach a rocky overlook where the valley and mountains open up before you. To the left is Big Falls of Overall Run, dropping off a sheer ledge into the canyon below. Sit back for a while and suck in the view. If you wish to continue exploring the area, you can follow the trail down the steep path to the stream below, and then follow the stream up until you reach the base of Big Falls. This area is especially popular with rock climbers, who come to test their skills on the cliffs.

After you have had your fill of adventure and scenery, begin the long haul retracing your steps back to the parking lot. The hike to the falls is mostly downhill for the entire distance and relatively easy. It's the climb back that will test your endurance and trail worthiness, as you ascend 2,000 vertical feet back to the parking lot.

Big Falls of Overall Run (Joseph Rossbach).

Total hiking distance: *6.4 miles out and back.*

Total hiking time: *3-4 hours.*

Elevation gain: *2,000 feet.*

Directions to trailhead: *From Thornton Gap entrance station, take Skyline Drive north for 10.4 miles to the parking area on the left, a few hundred yards before Hogback Mountain Overlook (which is at milepost 20.9).*

Activities: Hiking, backcountry camping, rock climbing.

Access Points: Skyline Drive.

Entrance fees: Up to $15/vehicle; varies depending on time of year.

Best times of year: May-October.

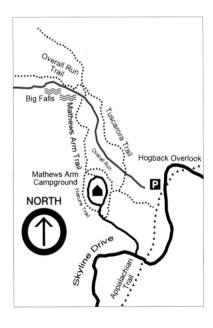

Calvert Cliffs
Calvert County, Maryland

Highlights: *Hunt for hand-sized teeth of the ancient super-shark megalodon beneath hundred foot high cliffs.*

When most people think of the Chesapeake Bay, they think of endless salt marshes and sandy beaches barely poking above the high tide line. Not many people think of towering cliffs or giant 50-foot sharks. But Maryland's Calvert County, on the western shore of the Chesapeake Bay, has them both—sort of.

The Calvert Cliffs formation dominates the Chesapeake's shoreline for over forty miles in Calvert County. The cliffs formed over 15 million years ago when all of southern Maryland was covered by a warm, shallow sea. Over 600 species of fossils have been identified from these cliffs, with shark teeth being the most abundant. Every now and then, someone finds a tooth of ancient Megalodon, a fearsome Pleistocene epoch apex predator. Megalodon was basically a giant great white shark, so just imagine the most fearsome predator swimming the oceans today and multiply it by three!

This paddle takes you past a particularly scenic stretch of cliffs to a wild beach and Parker's Creek, a beautiful tidal stream

Fossilized shark tooth (Ian Plant).

protected by the American Chestnut Land Trust. A sea kayak makes the ideal vessel for this trip—canoes may have trouble in the open waters of the Bay if the wind or waves are up at all. Launch from Breezy Point Marina, and when you get to the Bay, head right (south). Along the way you will pass several large sections of cliffs, some rising as high as two hundred feet. Feel free to stop along the way to explore the cliffs and look for fossils. Be careful when walking beneath the cliffs, as the soft clay is unstable and rock slides can occur. Notice the interesting geology of the cliffs, which are dominated by alternating

Calvert Cliffs at dawn (Ian Plant).

layers of blue and yellow clay. If you are interested in shark fossils, search in the surf zone. When waves come in, they sometimes churn up shark teeth fossils. If you find one as big as your hand, you know you have found a Megalodon tooth!

When you are ready, continue south. About four miles into your paddle you will pass Dares Beach, the largest community you will encounter on this trip. About one mile after Dares Beach, you'll reach Parkers Creek, which is an obvious large tidal creek flowing through a broad valley between the cliffs. There is a beautiful beach at Parkers Creek, a perfect place to stop for lunch. Note that the beach is home to the endangered tiger beetle, so please keep below the mean high tide line.

You can paddle up Parkers Creek for about a mile, exploring its many meanders. When you are ready, turn around and head back north to your launch at Breezy Point. Just don't get eaten by megalodon on the way back!

Total paddling distance: *10-12 miles round trip.*

Total paddling time: *4-5 hours.*

Paddling conditions: *Shallow but open tidal water, which can get choppy in rough weather.*

Directions: *From the Capital Beltway, take Route 4 south. After about 14 miles, take Route 260 east toward Chesapeake Beach for nine miles. When you reach Chesapeake Beach, you will arrive at a T-intersection with Route 261; turn right. Continue on Route 261 for several miles until you turn left on to Breezy Point road, which takes you to the Marina.*

Activities: Paddling, fossil collecting.

Access Points: Chesapeake Beach, Maryland.

Entrance fees: $10 boat launch fee.

Best times of year: Any.

Other places to see the Cliffs: Bayfront Park, just south of Chesapeake Beach on Route 261, is a great place to explore the cliffs on foot. This hike is best done at low tide; during high tide it can be impossible to walk beneath the cliffs. Make sure to arrive just before sunrise to witness a beautiful Chesapeake dawn!

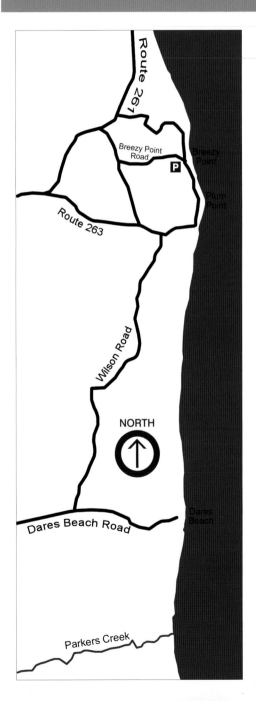

Potomac Whitewater
C&O Canal National Historic Park, Maryland

Highlights: *A thrilling but easy whitewater paddle down a side channel of the Potomac River.*

Are you looking for some excitement, but not *too* much? Then this scenic little stretch of easy whitewater is perfect for you! This paddle takes you across the Potomac River down a whitewater run in the Patowmack Canal, an old abandoned canal that parallels the river and that has been reclaimed by nature. There are even a few scenic islands along the way that make perfect backcountry camping destinations. The best thing about this trip is that no car shuttle is required. How, you may ask, can one paddle down a river but somehow end up back where one started? All will be revealed, in good time . . .

The whitewater you will encounter on this paddle is fairly easy, and can be attempted by anyone who is comfortable steering a canoe or kayak. Even easy whitewater can be dangerous, however. Make sure you wear a personal flotation device, and wear appropriate clothing for the weather (in cooler weather a wetsuit would be a good idea). If you capsize, keep your feet high and pointed downstream to avoid getting your legs caught by the current on an underwater rock or tree limb. Wait until the current slows before standing up in the water. This run is best done when the river levels are neither exceptionally high nor low; late spring and early summer are probably ideal. Check the USGS Potomac River gauge for Little Falls before starting (http://waterdata.usgs.gov/usa/nwis/uv ?site_no=01646500); the best conditions are when the gauge is between 3.4 and 4 feet. When the river is above four feet, this run can get dangerous; below 3 feet, the water may be too low for the rapids to be any good.

From the parking area, carry your canoe or kayak across the C&O Canal lock and then down to the Potomac River. Launch and head across the river, staying to the right (east) of a series of downstream rapids formed by the crumbling remains of an old dam. You are aiming for an opening on the Virginia side of the river just above the rapids. This is an entrance into the old canal, which was owned in part by George Washington.

Enter into the canal and let the current take you downstream. For a while, the water is sluggish as you pass under a canopy of tall green trees. Soon the current will pick up, and you will pass through small rapids and riffles as you continue to head down river.

Keep an eye out for downed trees—these will be the most significant water hazards you will encounter. Swing around them as much as you can; your boat can get pinned against or beneath such snags, and you can have a tough time getting unstuck!

The canal bifurcates several times. Try to pick the widest channel each time, but if you cannot don't worry, as the channels all lead to the same place. At times there will be side channels leading back to the Potomac; avoid these and keep within the canal. Eventually the current slackens before the canal merges with the river.

Once back in the Potomac, angle slightly upstream past several islands. These island, by the way, are great places to stop, rest, or explore. Several scenic gravel

Activities: Canoeing, kayaking, backcountry camping.

Access Points: Potomac, Maryland.

Entrance fees: None.

Best times of year: Summer.

beaches beckon, and there are a number of informal campsites that would make great overnight destinations. Past the islands, continue to angle slightly upstream and cross back to the Maryland side of the Potomac. You are aiming for a small, well-used beach. Once at the beach, carry your boat a few dozen feet to the C&O Canal. Ah, you say, so *here's* the answer to the question of how one can travel downstream and end up right back where one started! Indeed, take the canal left (east) for about a mile of scenic flat water paddling back to the parking area, A perfectly relaxing way to end an exciting and adventure-filled day.

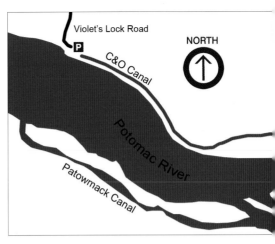

Total paddling distance: *2-3 miles round trip.*

Total paddling time: *1-2 hours.*

Paddling conditions: *Easy whitewater; hazards include downed trees.*

Directions to boat launch: *From the Capital Beltway, take Route 190 (River Road) west. Travel 11.3 miles, passing through the town of Potomac along the way, until you reach Violet's Lock Road. Follow the road to its end at a large parking area.*

Sunset over the Potomac River (Ian Plant).

Annapolis Rocks
Appalachian Trail, Maryland

Highlights: *Awesome mountain views along a scenic stretch of the magnificent Appalachian Trail.*

Maryland lays claim to only 40 miles of the 2,168 miles the Appalachian Trail runs from Georgia to Maine. Don't be discouraged, for what it lacks in length it makes up for in scenic grandeur. Running mostly along the spine of South Mountain, the AT passes a few great scenic locations, including two superlative overlooks: Annapolis Rocks and Black Rock.

Start the hike by crossing Route 40 and pick up the blue-blazed trail heading into the woods. At 0.1 mile, turn onto the white-blazed AT, and begin to follow the trail uphill away from the highway and the sounds of civilization. After one mile of hiking, you reach the summit of Pine Knob and the top of South Mountain. At this point, the trail levels off and continues for another mile to the intersection with a side trail that leads for 0.2 miles to Annapolis Rocks.

Annapolis Rocks offer impressive west facing views of Greenbrier Lake and the Cumberland Valley, as well as of four states (Maryland, Pennsylvania, West Virginia and Virginia). The quartzite crags are littered with boulders and small caves which are fun to explore. If you choose to camp here for the night, there are many nice campsites within the vicinity of the cliffs, and a small spring for filtering water. This is a great spot to sit and watch the sun set, and wait for the stars to appear in the darkening sky above.

Heading back to the AT, continue north for another mile until you reach Black Rock cliffs, just 40 feet off the trail to your left. The view from Black Rock cliffs is just as impressive as that from Annapolis Rocks, and on certain days you can spy hawks and vultures catching thermals over the Cumberland Valley below, in search of prey and carrion. At the base of Black Rock cliffs is a huge scree field of boulders and rocks that have fallen from the cliffs over the millennium. After soaking in the views, return back along the way you came to the parking lot.

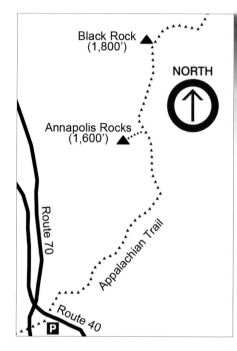

For those looking to extend this adventure from a day hike to an overnight, you can continue past Black Rock summit and hike all the way up to Pen Mar Gap at the Mason-Dixon line, 17.8 miles one-way

Activities: Hiking, backpacking.

Access Points: Myersville, Maryland.

Entrance fees: None.

Best times of year: Anytime.

Sunset over Annapolis Rocks (Ian Plant).

from the trailhead. Along the way you will pass the Devil's Racecourse, a field of large boulders with a small stream running through it, and High Rock, another rocky crag with great views of the surrounding countryside. Hemlock Hill Shelter, 8.2 miles into the hike, is the best spot to stop for the night. The shelter is clean and well built, with a privy and small spring for filtering water. A two-car shuttle will be required for this optional hike. Parking at the north end is available at Pen Mar County Park (inquire within about parking, and let park officials know you will be leaving your car there overnight; there is also parking available outside the park).

Total hiking distance: *6.4 miles round trip.*

Total hiking time: *3-4 hours.*

Elevation gain: *550 feet.*

Directions to trailhead: *From Route 70 heading west, take the Myersville Exit. Turn right on Wolfsville Road (Route 17), then make a left on Route 40. There is parking on the left for the Appalachian Trail, just before the Route 70 overpass.*

A Paddle for all Seasons
Mason Neck, Virginia

Highlights: *Experience different wildlife and scenery with each passing season on this pleasant Potomac River paddle.*

The Mason Neck peninsula is a tranquil island of relative wilderness adrift in a sea of urban sprawl. Most of the land on the peninsula is either federal, state, or county park land, and a substantial portion of the surrounding area is largely undeveloped. The boot-shaped peninsula is home to Elizabeth Hartwell Mason Neck National Wildlife Refuge and Mason Neck State Park, which were set aside to protect bald eagle habitat, as well as Pohick Bay Regional Park, another area popular with eagles. Eagles aren't the only wildlife you'll find here; in fact, Mason Neck is a veritable hot spot for a number of species including tundra swans, great blue herons, seagulls, osprey, mergansers—the list goes on. In fact, every season seems to bring a different group of animals to Mason Neck, which is why we recommend trying this paddle four times a year!

In winter, bald eagles and tundra swans converge on the area in large numbers. One large flock of about 80 tundra swans comes every winter to Mason Neck, and in

January and February the resident eagle population is joined by several dozen winter migrants. Come spring, hundreds of great blue herons and osprey replace the tundra swans and many of the eagles (don't worry, there's plenty of eagles left year round!); in fact, one of the largest heron rookeries on the east coast is found on the peninsula. Summer brings great egrets in large numbers, and young eagles and osprey begin to stretch their wings. In autumn, ducks and mergansers start to arrive as fall color begins to peak.

Although parts of this paddle can be done separately as round trips, to truly experience the wonder of Mason Neck, arrange a two-car shuttle, leaving one car at Mason Neck State Park, and launch your boats from Pohick Bay Regional Park. Once you have launched from Pohick (there is a small craft launch at the end of the boat launch parking lot), head east up Pohick Bay and explore its far tidal reaches. To your north is Fort Belvoir, some of which has been set aside as wilderness preserve open to the public. Large numbers of eagles congregate on Pohick Bay, especially in the winter, when up to several dozen eagles can be seen at one time.

After exploring Pohick, head southeast. Soon the shoreline will be dotted with homes, many of which are among the most expensive properties in Fairfax County. Although it is interesting to see how the "other half" lives, you'll be anxious to get back to wilderness, which you do shortly after rounding Hallowing Point. When the houses end, there will be a large tidal marsh to the north. This is the Great Marsh. Head into its shallow waters and find yourself enveloped in wilderness again. Beavers are very active here, and river otters are occasionally spotted. During the winter, tundra swans often gather here in large numbers.

Activities: Canoeing, kayaking, hiking.

Access Points: Lorton, Virginia.

Entrance fees: Pohick Bay Regional Park is $7 per vehicle (Alexandria, Arlington, City of Fairfax, Fairfax County, Falls Church and Loudoun residents can enter for free) plus a $9 launch fee ($4 for the above-mentioned residents). Mason Neck State Park is $3 weekdays, $4 weekends.

Best times of year: Any. Bald eagles and tundra swans peak in January and early February; great blue herons peak in April and May.

Bald eagle (Ian Plant).

After the Great Marsh, continue heading west. When you round the bottom of the "boot," you will soon come to the great blue heron rookery, which contains several hundred nests (although only a few dozen may be visible from the water). Do not attempt to enter the heron rookery during the nesting season; herons are skittish and have been known to abandon nesting areas *en masse* as the result of an intrusion. Rather, stay in your boat and enjoy the sights and sounds of hundreds of nesting herons.

Heading north past the rookery, you will soon enter the placid waters of Belmont Bay. After passing the boat launch at the state park, head into Kane's Creek for one last bit of exploration. Kane's Creek is a beautiful tidal creek filled with spatterdock. When done, head back to the boat launch to end your journey. If you aren't tired yet, there are many excellent hiking trails in the state park and the national wildlife refuge, as well as in Pohick Bay Regional Park.

Total paddling distance: *15-18 miles one way.*

Total paddling time: *8-10 hours.*

Paddling conditions: *Ranging from protected marsh to open, tidal water, which can get choppy in rough weather.*

Directions to Pohick Bay Regional Park: *From 95 south, take exit 163 to Lorton. At the end of the ramp take a left onto Lorton Road. Go under the second overpass and turn right onto Lorton Market Street. In about 1.5 miles you will reach a traffic light at Route 1 (Richmond Highway). Go straight through the light; the road becomes Gunston*

Road. You will reach the park entrance in about four miles on your left. The boat launch is at the end of the road to the left.

Directions to Mason Neck State Park: *Continuing past Pohick Bay Regional Park, after about one mile you will see a sign for Mason Neck State Park and the National Wildlife Refuge on your right. Take the right into the park, following the road past the gatehouse all the way to the visitor center. The boat launch is located just before the visitor center, off a short side road to the left.*

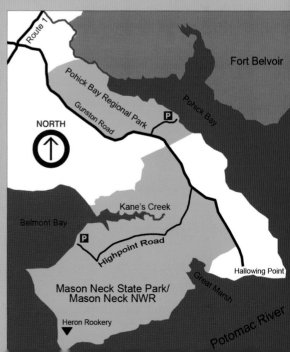

FARTHER AFIELD

Blackwater Falls in autumn (Joseph Rossbach).

16

Big Schloss
George Washington National Forest,
Virginia/West Virginia

Highlights: *A moderately strenuous hike to great views and interesting geology.*

Total hiking distance: *4.4 miles.*

Total hiking time: *2-3 hours.*

Elevation gain: *1,000 feet.*

Directions to trailhead: *From Route 81, take Exit 283 towards Woodstock. After exiting, take a right on Route 42. Follow Route 42 until Columbia Furnace. Once there, take a right onto Route 675; take Route 675 all the way to Wolf Gap Campground.*

Big Schloss was named by German immigrants who thought the peak looked like a giant castle looming over the valleys below. One look at the rocky summit is all you need to see why: with steep cliff faces, rock spires, and stone columns, it does in fact resemble an ancient, decaying castle. Big Schloss provides wonderful views in all directions of endless rolling mountains and quiet farmland. The interesting summit geology is a nice bonus, making this a superlative hike.

Starting at the Wolf Gap Campground, hike up the orange-blazed **Mill Mountain Trail**. The start of the trail is actually the steepest part of the hike. After about a mile, you will reach the top of a ridge line that leads to the summit. Turn left, and continue following the ridge for another mile before arriving at the junction of the white-blazed **Big Schloss Trail**. Turning right onto the trail will lead you another 0.3 miles to the summit, crossing a wooden bridge along the way.

What tremendous views! Take some time to soak in the scenery. For the more adventurous, consider camping near the summit to watch the Milky Way trace its path across the night sky. There is no water at the summit so bring plenty with you. To return, just retrace your route back to Wolf Gap Campground.

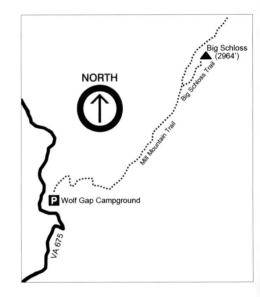

Activities: Hiking, backpacking.

Access Points: Wolf Gap Campground.

Entrance fees: None.

Best times of year: Spring through autumn.

Above: autumn view of Big Schloss. Right: stars over Big Schloss' summit (both pictures Ian Plant).

17

Cranesville Swamp
Cranesville Swamp Preserve, Maryland

Highlights: A slice of the Canadian tundra right here in the greater D.C. area.

In the Appalachian Mountains, bordering West Virginia and Maryland, west of Deep Creek Lake, is Cranesville Swamp. Tucked away in a frost pocket, Cranesville Swamp is an ecological wonderland. Just three miles long and a half-mile wide, Cranesville packs a great amount of biodiversity into such a small tract of land. Owned and maintained by the Nature Conservancy, Cranesville Swamp is home to a diverse collection of flora and fauna. Many rare species, including the tamarisk and sundew (a carnivorous, insect eating plant), are found in the swamp.

The average elevation of the swamp is 2,500 feet, with the uplands surrounding it reaching to 2,900 feet. Cranesville receives plenty of rain, on average 60 inches per year and can get triple that amount of snow, close to 160 inches per year. You may even find traces of snow in the early summer months. Muddy Creek and its famous falls, Maryland's tallest waterfall, finds its headwaters in the swamp.

Taking a trip to Cranesville Swamp is a trip back in time (geological time that is), reaching back 10,000 years into the last great Ice Age. As the glaciers made their advance south, conifer and fir forests moved ahead of them, over the course of thousands of years, and found a home in the Appalachian Mountains. The environment was much colder back then, and these plant communities, which normally exist in northern New England and Canada, found the perfect home in the mountains of the Mid-Atlantic. As the temperatures gradually warmed and the ice sheets retreated back to the north, the plant species that found their home here also slowly retreated back towards Canada. In a few places like Cranesville Swamp and Dolly Sods to the north, these northern communities lingered in some isolated "islands" and still exist today.

A 1,500 foot boardwalk and four walking trails provide a great opportunity to discover the many plant, animal and avian species that live in the swamp. A hike in Cranesville is not about elevation gain or long distances, but rather a chance to slow down and explore the many plant species. A walk along the wooden boardwalk passes through many different ecosystems, including sphagnum bogs lush with floating carpets of moss and rare plants such as the sundew, pitcher plant and skunk cabbage. As the boardwalk continues you will pass through blueberry and chokeberry, as well as taller shrubs including serviceberry, wild raisin and arrow wood.

A hike along the Blue Trail will put you into a stand of hemlock and pine that is a perfect place to spot some common and

Activities: Hiking.

Access Points: Lake Ford, Maryland.

Entrance fees: None.

Best times of year: Spring, fall, and winter.

Above & left: Cranesville Swamp has a diversity of plant life (both pictures Joseph Rossbach).

rare birds. Look out for great horned owl, screech owl and barred owl. Many other birds are known to inhabit the park, including great blue heron, ruby-throated hummingbird, belted kingfisher, tree swallow and many, many more. All four trails and the boardwalk can be combined into a longer loop hike that will give you a chance to see all the best that Cranesville Swamp has to offer.

Total hiking distance: *Depending on which trails you hike; each trail is less than two miles long.*

Total hiking time: *Allow several hours to fully explore the preserve.*

Elevation gain: *None.*

Directions to trailhead: *From Frederick, Maryland, take Route 70 west and go 52 miles; merge on to Route 68 towards Cumberland. Follow Route 68 for 76 miles and take exit 4 (Route 42) towards Friendsville. Follow Route 42 for 1.7 miles and turn left onto Blooming Rose Road. After 1.8 miles turn left at Trap Run Road. Follow Trap Run Road for 2.8 miles and then turn left onto White Rock Road. After 1.4 miles make a*

slight right at Cranesville Road. After 5 miles, at the Methodist Church, turn on to Lake Ford Road, and follow the Nature Conservancy signs to the parking area.

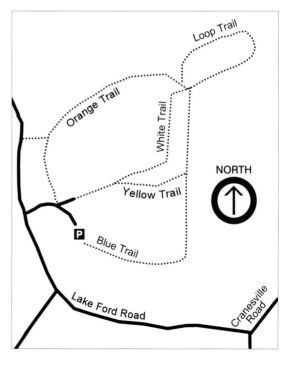

18

Lotus Bloom
Turner's Creek, Maryland

Highlights: *Paddle through the heart of the D.C. area's oldest and largest single living organism.*

Nelumbo lutea, the American Lotus, called yanquapin by Native Americans, is a colony plant that favors secluded tidal waterways. In summer, their showy white flowers tower over the tidal backwaters of the Sassafras River on Maryland's Eastern Shore, near where the river flows into the Chesapeake Bay.

Paddling through a lotus colony is—for lack of a better description—really cool.

Lotus is an "emergent" aquatic plant, meaning that while its roots are anchored in the mud, its large blue-green circular leaves and head-sized flowers emerge above the water's surface. This means that you can literally paddle under a lotus plant. Making the experience even cooler is the fact that lotus have an unusual

Other places to see wild lotus: American lotus occurs in protected coves of only a handful of creeks and rivers in the greater D.C. area. Some other lotus locations include: Mattawoman Creek (Indian Head, MD) and Wildwood Lake Sanctuary (Harrisburg, PA).

method of reproduction. Its seeds may remain dormant for more than a century before they germinate. When a seed germinates, the plant sends out underground stems (called rhizomes) that produce new, genetically identical plants. Consequently, a "population" of lotus can actually be a single—yet ridiculously enormous—plant. And by ridiculously enormous we mean acres in size, as much as a mile of lotus flowers and leaves connected by a network of rhizomes. So that means you get to paddle, not so much under the lotus plant, but rather *through* it. As we said, really cool.

After launching your kayak or canoe, proceed south into Turner's Creek for your first lotus experience. When you enter the huge lotus colony, you may find the paddling a little tricky as you fight your way through a jungle of tall plants. Skirting the edges is always an easier way to travel. Explore Turner's Creek for a while, and then head back past the boat launch and out into the open waters of the Sassafras River. Boat traffic and winds can sometimes make for choppy conditions, so be more careful than you would have been in the protected waters of Turner's Creek.

Heading west (left) around the bend of the river, after a mile from the boat launch you will notice a nice beach with an inlet leading to a lotus-filled pond. This is a great place to stop. The water in the inlet is shallow, and you should be able to ex-

Activities: Paddling, hiking.

Access Points: Turner's Creek Park, Maryland.

Entrance fees: None.

Best times of year: July and August.

Above & right: lotus flowers along Turner's Creek (both pictures Ian Plant).

plore much of the lotus colony here on foot if you like. Head back to the boat launch when you have had your fill.

Further exploration of the Sassafras River by boat is possible; this stretch of the River is very scenic and largely undeveloped. Heading west, the river empties into the Chesapeake Bay about five miles from the boat launch.

You can also hike in the nearby Sassafras Natural Resource Management Area. One of the trails will take you to the river's edge; turn right and walk along the shore until you reach the lotus pond.

Total paddling distance: *4-5 miles.*

Total paddling time: *2-3 hours.*

Difficulty: *Mostly flat water.*

Directions to boat launch: *From the Chesapeake Bay Bridge, head east on Route 50 to Route 301 North. In 6 miles, take Route 213 north to Chestertown. Continue past Chestertown on Route 213 for 10 miles and turn left on Route 298. Travel approximately 2 miles and turn*

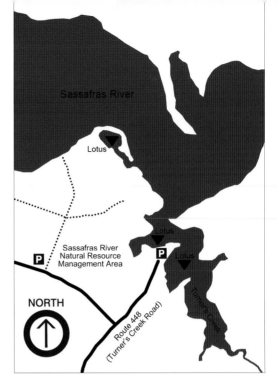

right on Route 448 (Turner's Creek Road). Drive three miles to the boat ramp. Parking for the hiking area is on a dirt side road about three-quarters of a mile before the launch.

19

New Point Comfort
Mathews County, Virginia

Highlights: *Miles of wild beaches and salt marsh to explore, abundant wildlife, and an historic white stone lighthouse—and oh yeah, no crowds!*

Mathews County, tucked away on the western shore of the Chesapeake Bay in Virginia, has over 200 miles of shoreline on only 87 square miles of land. Why is this important? It means that there are many nooks and crannies for the intrepid paddler to explore, and the chance to lose oneself in a classic and especially scenic Chesapeake wilderness.

Mathews Blueways Water Trail, an interconnected system of ninety miles of water trails spanning the waters of Mathews County, winds its way through salt marshes, small islands, and sandy beaches. The sparsely developed shoreline and historic buildings (including an old tide mill, steamship wharves, and quaint fishing villages) add charm to the natural setting, and miles of wild beach encourage an escape from the realities of modern life.

The paddling in Mathews County is, quite simply, exceptional. Sea and touring kayaks are the best craft for paddling the open waters of the Chesapeake Bay, as they are faster and more stable than canoes, although canoes can be appropriate for exploring salt marsh or protected harbors. There can be strong winds and steep waves on some sections of the Blueways Trail when the weather is bad. If you are planning on an extended trip, make sure you know what you are doing.

The highlight of the Blueways Trail is New Point Comfort Preserve, which is a wild beach that looks straight into the Chesapeake's third oldest—and arguably most beautiful—lighthouse. New Point Comfort

Lighthouse rests on an island off of the southern tip of New Point Comfort, and is made of white stone.

New Point Comfort Preserve can be reached by a short paddle, or as part of a longer paddle or an extended trip. The preserve contains a white sand beach, great views, shorebirds of all kinds (including gulls, terns, black skimmers, and pelicans), and not much more. "Leave No Trace" camping is allowed on the preserve; just be sure to leave the beach as unspoiled as you found it. If you opt for an overnight stay, you will be lulled to sleep by the peaceful sound of wind, waves, and the calls of seabirds.

Activities: Kayaking and canoeing.

Access Points: Bavon, Virginia.

Entrance fees: None.

Best times of year: Spring, late summer through autumn.

There are two launch points that are relatively close to New Point Comfort. One is Davis Creek Landing off of Route 689. It is about a half mile from the launch to the open waters of Mobjack Bay; turning left it is another two miles to the preserve. The other launch point, New Point Comfort Landing off of Route 600, is about a mile away from the preserve, a bit longer if one chooses to explore upstream into Harper

Creek before heading to the lighthouse. Whether launching from either location, your destination is fairly clear—head for the gleaming white stone lighthouse. Trips to the lighthouse itself add a little extra distance; as of this writing it is permissible to land on the lighthouse island, but the lighthouse interior is closed to all public access.

For an extended adventure, consider several days of paddling, either working from a base camp (such as one of the many excellent bed & breakfasts in Mathews County), or backcountry camping. There is no shortage of beautiful things to see in this quiet little corner of the Chesapeake.

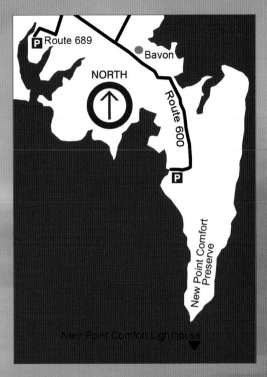

Total paddling distance: *From Davis Creek Landing, 6-8 miles; from New Point Comfort Landing, 2-3 miles. Longer trips can be taken.*

Total paddling time: *From Davis Creek Landing, 3-4 hours; from New Point Comfort Landing, 1-2 hours.*

Paddling conditions: *Ranging from sheltered water to open water. High winds and waves are possible.*

Directions to boat launch: *From Route 17 in Gloucester County, take Route 14 to the town of Gloucester. Follow signs for Route 14 to the town of* *Mathews. Continue on Route 14 until Shadow. For access to the Davis Creek Landing, turn right on to Route 600, and then take another right to Route 689, which ends at the boat launch. For New Point Comfort Landing, continue on Route 600 until the end, where there is a boat launch and a viewing deck.*

Sunrise light over New Point Comfort Lighthouse (Ian Plant).

20

Morris Creek
Chickahominy Wildlife Management Area, Virginia

Highlights: *Paddle through the swamp where famous explorer Captain John Smith was captured!*

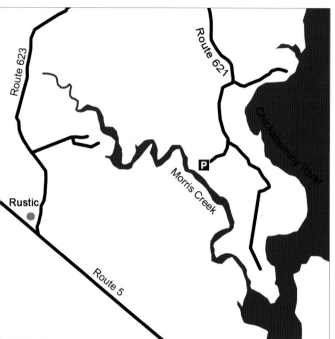

From the boat launch, head upstream to explore the cypress-lined banks of Morris Creek. When you've gone as far as you can go, head downstream to the confluence of Morris Creek and the Chichahominy before heading back to your vehicle. There are plenty of places to stop along the way, to admire the scenery or to just take a break from paddling. For the most part you will be surrounded by wilderness. Late autumn is a particularly good time to explore the creek; the cypress needles will be ablaze with crimson by the first week of November. Longer trips are possible, venturing into the Chickahominy and exploring its many scenic tidal tributaries.

Total paddling distance: *8-9 miles.*

Total paddling time: *3-4 hours.*

Difficulty: *Flat water.*

Directions to boat launch: *From Route 5 south, take a left (north) on Route 623 near Rustic, VA. After about 4 miles, take a right onto Route 621. In just under 3 miles, you will arrive at a cul-de-sac. Take a right on a gravel road, follow it for .8 miles, bear right where the road splits, reaching the boat launch in another half mile.*

Over 400 years ago, famous adventurer Captain John Smith was scouting near Morris Creek when he was ambushed and captured by soldiers in Chief Powhatan's army. Powhatan ordered Smith executed, but before the deed could be done, the chief's daughter, Pocahontas, intervened on Smith's behalf, saving his life. Or at least that's the story according to John Smith, who unfortunately was known to tell a whopper or two in his lifetime!

Historians may doubt Smith's account, but there can be no doubt that Morris Creek is a place of serene beauty. Morris Creek is a backwater tidal creek of the Chichahominy River, lined with majestic bald cypress trees and fields of marsh grass. It makes a perfect place to canoe or kayak, and there are even opportunities for backcountry camping in the surrounding wildlife management area.

Right: Morris Creek cypress (Ian Plant).

Activities: Canoeing, kayaking, backcountry camping.

Access Points: Rustic, Virginia.

Entrance fees: None.

Best time of year: Spring through fall.

21

Smith Island
Smith Island, Maryland

Highlights: *Paddle through a historic island where time stands still to visit an amazing summer bird colony.*

Smith Island is an isolated island community miles from the mainland, reachable only by passenger ferry. Three small towns are on the island—Ewell, Tylerton, and Rhodes Point—home to a once thriving "waterman" economy, based on fishing, crabbing, and harvesting oysters. Now, times are a bit tough for the Chesapeake waterman, and the three communities have shrunk somewhat from their heyday. Less than 400 people live on the island today.

Of all the trips in this book, this one is the most challenging from a logistical point of view. It is also one of the most rewarding. Every summer, thousands of pelicans, cormorants, and gulls come to nest on a remote, uninhabited island within the Smith Island group. It is one of the most incredible wildlife events in the Mid-Atlantic area!

Getting to the island is the trickiest part. Although skilled paddlers can kayak six miles from the mainland over open water to reach Smith Island, for most people the best way to get to the island is by taking a passenger ferry. Either bring kayaks or canoes with you on the ferry, or plan to rent them once on the island. Although sea kayaks are best as they give you the versatility to paddle not only the island's protected inland marshes but also around its outer edges, canoes work fine for exploring the tidal marshes.

Because the ferry schedule leaves you little time for exploration on a day trip, it is best to stay at least one night on Smith Island—or better yet, several. There is lodging available in Ewell and Tylerton. Both communities are very small, with several dozen houses and small businesses clustered around the town docks. Dining options are somewhat limited, especially in Tylerton. Just make sure that wherever you eat, you try some locally harvested blue crabs, and end your meal with some famous Smith Island ten-layer cake! What both towns have in abundance is solitude, and a sense of getting away from it all.

One can easily spend several days exploring Smith Island's maze of tidal marshes and bay-side beaches. The trip described here is from Tylerton to the bird nesting colony. If you are based in Ewell, you will have to first travel to Tylerton, which is easily accomplished following the main channel cutting through the heart of the island for about two miles.

From the beautiful waterfront of Tylerton, head southwest and follow a marked kayak trail with orange signs atop white PVC poles. This will take you south and west through a break in the salt marsh. Take the channel until you reach open water again, and head south once more. You will see power lines coming out of the water stretching from north to south for miles; they will parallel your journey on your right. On your way, keep a sharp eye out for osprey, bald eagles, great blue and tri-colored herons, terns, great and snowy egrets, as well as many other species that inhabit the marsh. As you paddle along, you can't help but notice how low and flat the land is; the highest ground is just a few feet above sea level.

Activities: Kayaking and canoeing.

Access Points: Crisfield, Maryland.

Entrance fees: Parking for ferry ($3); ferry ride ($40 round trip); additional fee for transporting kayaks or canoes.

Best times of year: June through August.

Cormorant chicks at dawn (Ian Plant).

Brown pelican feeding chick (Ian Plant).

You are heading for a small spit of barrier beach a few miles south of Tylerton. It's pretty hard to miss; eventually you will see a large number of brown pelicans and other birds congregating in one area. This is the summer nesting colony! You might not have noticed, but at some point you have actually left Maryland and crossed over into Virginia.

As you approach, you will observe that the beach is covered with hundreds, if not thousands, of brown pelicans. If you plan to land, pick a spot where no birds are congregating—you don't want to disturb the nesting birds. The pelicans, gulls, and cormorants nest within the marsh grass behind the beach. In any event, don't stay long—the birds come back to this spot every year because they feel safe, but they won't feel that way anymore if hordes of kayakers stop here for a beach party.

From here, either head back or wander to your heart's content. To explore more, make sure to get a copy of the official guide to the island's many water trails.

Total paddling distance: *4-5 miles.*

Total paddling time: *3-4 hours.*

Difficulty: *Tidal water subject to strong wind and currents.*

Directions to Smith Island: *Passenger ferries leave twice daily to Smith Island from Crisfield, Maryland (during the summer season, ferry service also leaves from Point Lookout, Maryland and Reedville, Virginia). The "Captain Jason" and the "Island Belle" head to Ewell, whereas the "Captain Jason II" goes to Tylerton as well as Ewell. All ferries leave at 12:30 PM and 5:00 PM from the city dock, where Route 413 dead-ends at the water. Parking is available in Crisfield, either at the municipal lot on Route 413 (close to the ferries) or at the J.P Tawes Bros. Hardware store lot. There is a $3 charge for overnight parking in either location. Someone is usually stationed at the J.P. Tawes lot; if not inquire in the store about parking. The ferry ride takes 45 minutes to an hour. The ferries will transport you and your equipment, and kayaks as well for an additional small fee. During the winter and early spring months, it is best to check ahead of time with the ferry captains to make sure they will be running. Return trips from the island are at 7:00 AM and 3:30 PM. Lodging and dining are available in Ewell and Tylerton. Ewell, being the larger of the two towns, has more options. Rhodes Point is smaller than both and connected to Ewell by road. Travel between Ewell and Tylerton is only possible by boat.*

50 AMAZING THINGS

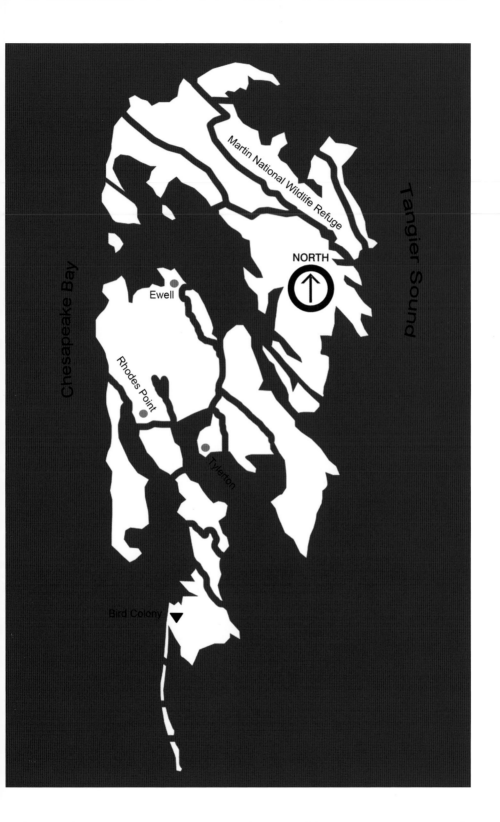

Martin National Wildlife Refuge

Tangier Sound

NORTH

Chesapeake Bay

Ewell

Rhodes Point

Tylerton

Bird Colony

22

Janes Island
Janes Island State Park, Maryland

Highlights: *Paddle through classic Chesapeake Bay salt marsh scenery and stroll along miles of wild beach.*

Janes Island is a magical place, an idyllic escape from the everyday hectic life. It is a place to lose yourself in a maze of salt marsh, or to walk for miles on a scenic beach that is completely undeveloped and uninhabited. It is a place to be surrounded on all sides by *wilderness*—a concept that is too often forgotten by the hordes of inhabitants of the greater D.C. metro area!

Janes Island State Park, located on the Eastern Shore of the Chesapeake Bay just outside of Crisfield, Maryland, preserves completely a giant island, protecting one of the last great classic Chesapeake landscapes. As the island is cut off completely from the mainland and reachable only by boat, you have a fair chance of having the whole place to yourself.

Much of the landward side of the island is a maze of small channels and salt marsh,

making it appropriate for canoe travel. Trips around the island head out into the unprotected waters of Tangier Sound, making a kayak the logical choice. Either way, you'll have miles and miles to

Activities: Kayaking and canoeing, backcountry camping.

Access Points: Crisfield, Maryland.

Entrance fees: None.

Best times of year: Early spring and late autumn.

explore. There are also several designated backcountry campsites; inquire at the park office for more information or to reserve a site.

Janes Island at sunset (Ian Plant).

With over 30 miles of water trails, there is no shortage of paddling opportunities. All of the park's water trails are marked with signs, but they can sometimes be a little hard to find and follow. Remember that the marshes of the island can be a maze of channels and inlets, so make sure your navigation skills are up to snuff before venturing too far; a GPS might come in handy as well.

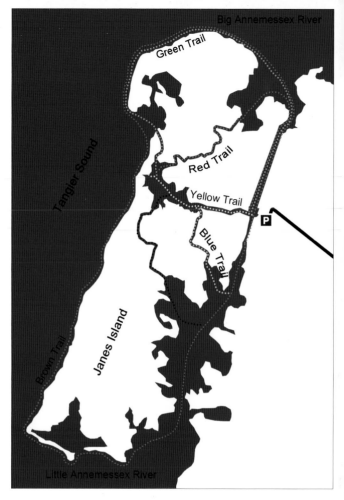

If you want a sampler of the best that Janes Island has to offer, try the **Green Trail**. After launching your boat, head north (right) up the channel and follow the Green Trail markers. After a little over one mile, you will exit into the Big Annemessex River. Head west (left) and follow the curving shore of Janes Island. Soon you will be in the open waters of Tangier Sound. The shoreline becomes sandy on the west side of the island, with plenty of places to stop and enjoy a nice swim.

The Green Trail leaves Tangier Sound and enters into an obvious channel leading into the salt marshes. You will soon join up with the **Yellow Trail** near the Janes Island dock, which is often covered with pelicans, cormorants, terns, and seagulls. Stop at the dock and take a stroll to the beach, walking to your heart's content. When ready to return to the mainland, follow the Yellow Trail east for a more or less straight shot back to the boat launch.

For the more adventurous, consider taking the 12.5-mile **Brown Trail** around the island. Or, just spend a day exploring the island's extensive salt marshes or walking along the beach—your pick!

Mosquitoes here are legendary. Avoid the park during the height of summer. The marshes in particular can be bad; the beaches not so much. Autumn or early spring can be good times to paddle here, or any day with a stiff breeze. Otherwise, bring bug netting and plenty of potent insect repellent!

Total paddling distance: *(Green/ Yellow Trail loop) 6-7 miles.*

Total paddling time: *4-6 hours.*

Difficulty: *A mix of protected and open water subject to high wind and waves.*

Directions to boat launch: *The park may be reached from Route 50 by taking Route 13 south to Westover, then taking Route 413 south approximately 11 miles to Plantation Road. Take a right and travel 1.5 miles to the park entrance.*

23

Snow Geese Explosion
Bombay Hook National Wildlife Refuge, Delaware

Highlights: *One of the greatest wildlife migrations in the Mid-Atlantic area, and one of the most impressive displays of raw animal power anywhere.*

Snow geese at sunset (Ian Plant).

In one of the great animal migrations on the planet, every fall a multitude of birds migrate through the Eastern Shore of Delaware, Maryland, and Virginia. Raptors, Canada geese, tundra swans, and ducks of every sort pass through the area, gathering in increasing numbers as autumn gives way to winter. But one event dwarfs them all—the arrival of tens of thousands of snow geese by mid-November, when their cacophonous gaggles darken the winter skies over the Delmarva Penninsula.

Arguably the best place to witness this migration is Bombay Hook National Wildlife Refuge in Delaware. A low marsh landscape tucked in a remote corner of the Delaware Bay tidewater area just north of Dover, every winter Bombay Hook plays host to as many as 200,000 snow geese. The geese begin to arrive in late October and sometimes stay as late as February and March before departing for their breeding grounds in the arctic. The geese usually peak from mid-November

through early January, and will sometimes linger in the area until early spring.

As impressive as seeing tens of thousands of brilliant white snow geese at one time, nothing compares to watching them suddenly explode into flight in unison, an event known as "liftoff." And understandably so, as it arguably compares in excitement to the launch of a rocket ship bound for space! Without warning, an entire flock will explode into the air, with the sound like a shotgun blast of several thousand wings suddenly beating at once. As the flock wheels through the sky overhead, their awe-inspiring numbers can even block the sun.

Snow geese landing (Ian Plant).

The refuge can be explored by car or bike. There are also a number of short hiking trails that lead to observation towers. The snow geese tend to congregate in several large flocks scattered throughout the refuge. Raymond Pool and Bear Swamp Pool seem to be favorite locations, but the flocks don't always stay in one place.

Activities: Wildlife watching, hiking, biking.

Access Points: Smyrna, Delaware.

Entrance fees: $4.00 per vehicle.

Best times of year: Mid-November through early January.

Liftoff, with a handful of tundra swans in the foreground (Ian Plant).

The best times to view liftoff are at sunrise and sunset. During the middle of the day, many geese fly away to feed in nearby farmers' fields, but they return to the refuge to spend the night, so their numbers are greatest from late afternoon to early morning. Plan to arrive two hours before sunset, or plan to arrive just before sunrise and to stay for an hour or two, to maximize your chances of seeing liftoff. Often, liftoff will occur not once but twice or even three times at sunrise or sunset. It is a heart-pounding event—you may even feel the urge to take flight yourself, but will find that breaking the earth's gravitational pull is rather difficult—so stay to watch as many liftoffs as you can. Just dress warm; the open marshes of the refuge can be a cold and windy place in winter, especially when waiting for liftoff.

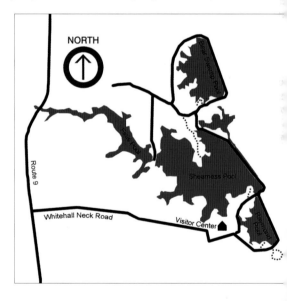

Directions to Refuge: *From Route 13 north of Dover, take Route 42 east toward Leipsic. Turn north on Route 9, and in a little over one mile turn east (right) on Whitehall Neck Road, which leads to the Refuge entrance. The Refuge is open from sunrise to sunset, although the gate is usually open before sunrise.*

Other places to watch snow geese: Blackwater National Wildlife Refuge in Maryland and Chincoteague National Wildlife Refuge in Virginia are also excellent places to view snow geese in large numbers.

24

Assateague Island
Assateague Island National Seashore, Maryland & Virginia

Highlights: *What's not to love about Assateague? Wildlife, wild ponies, sunrises to die for, and miles and miles of wild Atlantic shore.*

If you're looking for miles of unspoiled coastal beaches, a tremendous variety of wildlife, and great recreational opportunities, look no further than Assateague Island National Seashore. Assateague Island is a 37-mile long barrier island with pristine white beaches; wind sculpted barrier dunes; marsh lands; wild ponies; and thousands of migratory birds, including snow geese, piping plovers, great egrets, snowy egrets, Canada geese, double crested cormorants, tree swallows, and black crowned night herons—just to name a few.

Activities: Hiking, paddling.

Access Points: Ocean City, Maryland and Chincoteague, Virginia.

Entrance fees: $10/vehicle MD entrance; $5/ vehicle VA entrance.

Best times of year: November through May.

The island's most famous denizens are its world-renowned wild ponies. The ponies are actually stunted horses that have adapted to their environment, eating marsh grasses and drinking freshwater from small ponds. Their "barrel" appearance is a result of high salt content in their diet.

There are many recreational opportunities on the island. At the most basic level, one can simply head out to the beach for a stroll. Bird-watching is popular in particular at the Virginia entrance of the park, which passes through Chincoteague National Wildlife Refuge, where most of the island's bird population, and bird watchers, seem to reside.

To truly experience the wonder of the wilds of Assateague, consider a two-car shuttle, end-to-end hiking or paddling trip of the entire island. Canoes and kayaks are a great way to explore the protected waters behind the island, away from the pounding surf of the Atlantic. There are a number of backcountry campsites on the Maryland side of the island; the State Line and Pope Bay sites are both

Assateague's wild ponies (Ian Plant).

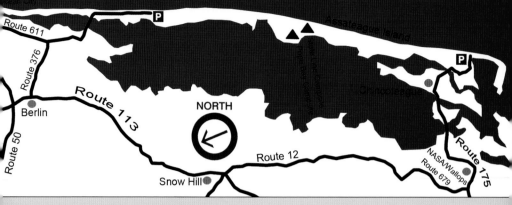

near the half-way point between the developed areas of the Maryland and Virginia sides, and either site makes a perfect and remote mid-point destination. If you wish to camp at any of the backcountry sites, you need to stop by the Maryland-side ranger station to obtain a permit ($5 per person) and to get information about where to park your shuttle vehicles on each side of the island.

It's about 13 miles on the Maryland side of the island until you reach the state line (marked by a fence that can be passed by hikers through a narrow gate), and another 12 miles after that before you reach the parking area on the Virginia side. To avoid a two-car shuttle, hike or paddle one way to the Pope Bay or State Line sites and go back the same way you came. There are also a number of intermediate destinations on the Maryland side (the Virginia side doesn't have any campsites). Note that there is no drinking water on the island, so plan to bring plenty of your own.

Total hiking/paddling distance: *25 miles one way.*

Total hiking/paddling time: *2 days.*

Paddling conditions: *Although the bay side waters are protected from the pounding surf of the Atlantic, things can still get a bit rough in windy conditions.*

Directions to Assateague: *There are two entrances to Assateague Island National Seashore. Assateague's north entrance is at the end of Route 611, eight miles south of Ocean City, MD. The south entrance is at the end of Route 175, two miles from Chincoteague, VA. There is no vehicle access between the two entrances on Assateague Island. Vehicles must return to the mainland to access either the north or south entrance.*

A wild Atlantic sunrise from Assateague Island (Ian Plant)

25

Big Dunes
Cape Henlopen State Park, Delaware

Highlights: *Huge dunes, wild Atlantic shore, coastal wetlands, and a view of a lighthouse all in one place.*

If you're in search of wild beaches, towering sand dunes, coastal wetlands and views of lighthouses, look no further than Cape Henlopen State Park. Situated on the Delaware Bay just east of Rehobeth, Cape Henlopen's 5,133 acres of natural beauty beckons the adventurous traveler to visit this coastal jewel.

You can explore this park on foot and get to some of the most notable and scenic locations after relatively short hikes. One of the best is the **Gordons Pond Trail**, which allows you to experience all the park has to offer. From the parking area, follow the trail around the south end of Gordon Pond and head north, keeping a keen eye out for wading birds fishing in the still waters. During the annual autumn and spring bird migrations, the

Activities: Hiking, beach-combing, wildlife watching.

Access Points: Rehobeth, Delaware.

Entrance fees: Up to $5 per vehicle.

Best times of year: Anytime. Late October and early November bring an impressive display of fall color.

view from the observation deck at Gordons Pond can be excellent.

The hike continues through a coastal pine forest as you head for Herring Point and the big sand dunes that the park is best known for. After two miles into the hike, you enter the dune field, with blueberry bushes and dune grass dotting the white sand landscape. Be aware that the dunes are a fragile environment and it is best to keep to the trail. Eventually you will reach Herring Point, with a great view of the beaches stretching north and south. From here enjoy a nice stroll down the beach for 1.5 miles to an access point that leads back to the trailhead.

Total hiking distance: *Four miles.*

Total hiking time: *2-3 hours.*

Elevation gain: *None.*

Directions to trailhead: *From Rehobeth, take 1st Street north until you reach Lake Avenue; turn right. Turn left onto Surf Avenue and follow to Henlopen Avenue/ Ocean Drive. Turn right and follow Ocean Drive to the park entrance. The trailhead starts from the left side parking lot.*

Cape Henlopen's wild shores (Joseph Rossbach).

NORTH

Nearby attractions: While you're in the area, you might consider riding the ferry across the bay to Cape May, New Jersey. Cape May has some amazing beaches that border the Delaware Bay and Atlantic Ocean, as well as a charming downtown with colorful Victorian homes. The Cape May Lighthouse is a popular place to visit, and you can explore the beaches along Cape May State Park. The Lewes-Cape May Ferry leaves from the town of Lewes, just outside of Henlopen State Park. The trip across is roughly 90 minutes. Check their website (www.capemaylewesferry.com) for costs and departure times.

26

Horseshoe Crab Spawn
Slaughter Beach, Delaware

Highlights: *One of the most breathtaking and incredibly weird wildlife events on the planet!*

All is calm on the shores of a great bay. The sun hangs over the horizon, ablaze in red as it awaits its final plunge into darkness. Nothing stirs save for the wind, waves, and tide. Suddenly, armored shapes appear in the rolling surf, moving slowly, inexorably, toward shore. By the thousands they come, grotesque and hideous soldiers at the van of a great invasion. They swarm the idyllic beach, overcoming everything in their path, their steely will focused on one single task.

An alien invasion? A scene from some prehistoric feeding frenzy? No, it's the annual Atlantic horseshoe crab spawn, one of the most amazing wildlife events on the planet! Every year, tens of thousands of horseshoe crabs come ashore on the beaches of the Delaware Bay to spawn, and if you are fortunate enough to be at the right place at the right time, you will witness crabs literally covering the entire shore for miles in all directions. This certainly is one of the most unique—and creepy—wildlife experiences in the Mid-Atlantic area.

There are many places to see the crabs in Delaware and New Jersey. Cape May on the New Jersey shore has many remote beaches for crab viewing, but unfortunately many of the New Jersey beaches are closed during prime crab spawning season to protect migrating birds. Most of the Delaware beaches, on the other hand, are easy to access and open year round. Arguably the best place to watch crabs is Slaughter Beach in Delaware. Simply drive into town, find parking, head for the beach, and wait!

Timing is critical if you wish to see a peak spawning event. Crab numbers peak during full and new moons between mid-May and late June. Two days prior through two days after each moon event offers the best chances of seeing peak crab activity. The crabs come ashore with the high tide, often just before sunset, to engage in their . . . ahem, activity . . . throughout the night. Crab numbers vary year-by-year; sometimes the crabs come ashore in the mere hundreds, and sometimes they come ashore in the thousands, covering the beach in all directions. So bring a flashlight, and keep your fingers crossed!

The crabs are not actually mating, they are spawning, which means that females lay eggs and then the males subsequently fertilize the eggs. But it sure doesn't look that way! A male will grasp a female's abdomen and hold on waiting for the female to lay her eggs, while "satellite" males follow the conjoined pair, so any single female usually has several males in tow. The result is that the crabs appear to be rolling all over each other, looking like a scene out of some mythic ancient Roman orgy, but in reality the whole affair is somewhat less kinky in nature.

The next morning the shore will be littered with hundreds of crabs, flipped upside down by waves and subsequently stranded by the receding tide. Those crabs that are unable to right themselves become food for migrating birds.

Activities: Beach-combing, wildlife watching.

Access Points: Slaughter Beach, Delaware (take Slaughter Beach road off of Coastal Highway Route 1).

Entrance fees: None.

Best times of year: May and June near the full or new moon.

A peak spawning year (Ian Plant).

27

Paddle with the Dolphins
Virginia Beach, Virginia

Highlights: *Sea kayak at sunrise or sunset with dolphins at the confluence of the Chesapeake Bay and the Atlantic Ocean.*

Everybody loves dolphins. Their playful antics and gravity-defying acrobatics are a thrill to watch. But why go to Sea World when you can see the real thing? Even better, why see the real thing when you can *experience* it? This paddle will put you in prime dolphin-watching waters; in fact, it might put you right in the middle of a dolphin pod!

Every summer (from June through October), hundreds of bottle-nosed dolphins come from the Atlantic to feed in the fish-rich waters at the mouth of the Chesapeake Bay. With an average size of between ten and twenty dolphins, pods range back and forth across the mouth of the Bay hunting for food. There's nothing quite like sea kayaking with a pod of dolphins, watching them as they swim, splash, and leap out of the water all around you. It is a heart-pounding experience, although in some part this is due to the fact that you have to paddle really fast to keep up with dolphins!

A sea kayak or a sit-on-top kayak is best for this paddle. The waters here are open and waves can sometimes be somewhat rough—this is, after all, practically the Atlantic Ocean. Canoes will have difficulty on all but the calmest days.

This paddle starts at the Lynnhaven Boat Ramp and Beach Facility. There is a fee for parking, but as of this writing it is free to launch a kayak. From the launch, head north (left) through the channel to the open waters of the Chesapeake Bay. Head east (right) when you exit the channel,

and keep your eyes peeled for dolphins. Within less than a mile, you will come to First Landing State Park, which owns the shore for the next half-mile or so (if you have some spare time before or after your paddle, head to the park's beautiful bald cypress forest, draped with eerie Spanish moss).

After First Landing, the shore is owned by Fort Story, a U.S. Army Transportation Corps installation. Access to Fort Story is restricted to base personnel and family, and visitors with a permit. Therefore, unless you meet these requirements, technically you are not allowed to land. Base security regularly patrols the beach. Although much of the Fort Story beachfront is usually filled with base personnel and their families sunbathing and swimming, making it appear to be a welcoming place, please respect the base rules and avoid landing unless it is really necessary. Feel free to land anywhere along First Landing State Park, although be aware that the demarcation between the state park and the army base is

Activities: Sea kayaking.

Access Points: Virginia Beach.

Entrance fees: Parking fee $4.

Best times of year: June through October.

Dolphin breaching (Ian Plant).

not always clear. Once you get to Fort Story, you should start seeing dolphins more regularly. Sunrise and sunset are particularly good for dolphin watching, as they seem to increase their feeding activity at these times. The dolphins will often fish close to shore, waving their tail flukes in the air when they are feeding. They almost seem to be playing as they leap and frolic, and they sometimes enjoy riding a kayaker's wake—if you can go fast enough to create one, that is. Remember that although they might seem unfazed by your presence, you should nonetheless avoid chasing or otherwise harassing dolphins.

When you get to the eastern tip of Cape Henry, begin heading back. For the more adventurous, consider heading south to further explore the coast. Be aware that you are now in the open Atlantic, and sea conditions may be rougher than the somewhat more protected waters of the Bay. As much of the shore is either private property or military installation, you may not find many places to land.

Total paddling distance: *6-10 miles round trip.*

Total paddling time: *3-4 hours.*

Paddling conditions: *Open water subject to high winds and waves.*

Directions to boat launch: *From US 60 in Virginia Beach (Shore Drive), turn right at East Stratford Road. Take an immediate left onto Piedmont Circle. Look for signs for the boat launch.*

Nearby attractions: In winter, the dolphins leave, only to be replaced by humpback and fin whales. Kayaking to see the whales is probably not a great idea, for several reasons. One, whales swim much faster than dolphins, and are difficult (impossible) to keep up with in a kayak. Two, the cold weather and water make for potentially dangerous conditions. Three, can you imagine a humpback whale suddenly lunge-feeding below your kayak?! Not to worry, as whale-watching tours leave Rudee Inlet on a regular basis from late December through early March. Contact the Virginia Aquarium and Marine Science Center in Virginia Beach for more information, tour schedules, and fees. During the summer, dolphin tours depart on a regular basis as well, but what's the fun in that?

Humpback whale lunge feeding (Ian Plant).

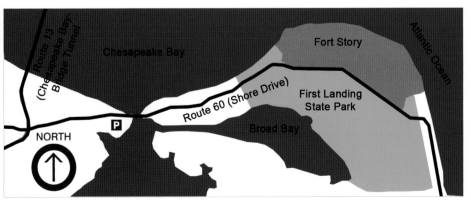

28

A Trip Back in Time
Lake Drummond, Great Dismal Swamp National Wildlife Refuge, Virginia

Highlights: *A glorious paddle to a hauntingly beautiful and completely wild natural lake with bald cypress, Spanish moss, and solitude.*

Twisted bald cypress trees rise eerily from the tannin-stained waters of a vast lake, Spanish moss clinging to their feathery needles. Waterfowl cries echo in the distance. Wilderness in all directions, as far as the eye can see. Louisiana? Florida? South Carolina? Nope, Virginia! Like a slice of the bayou, just without all those pesky gators.

Lake Drummond is one of two natural lakes in Virginia, and is quite easily one of the most beautiful and remote places in the Mid-Atlantic area. Bowl-shaped with acid-stained water (due to the organic acids leaching into the water from surrounding swamp and peat soils), Lake Drummond is fairly large (3,142 acres) but shallow (with a maximum depth of six feet). The origin of Lake Drummond is a mystery; some scientists believe water filled in the impact crater of a meteorite; others believe the lake was formed after a massive peat burn several thousand years ago. Today, the swamp surrounding the lake is home to many bird, reptile, and mammal species, including over 300 black bear.

The lake has an interesting history. It is named after William Drummond, the first governor of North Carolina, who was also the first European to explore the lake. In 1763, George Washington formed a company that purchased 40,000 acres of swampland surrounding the lake for the purpose of draining the swamp, harvesting the trees, and using the land for farming. Although Washington dug several ditches to drain the swamp and to transport logs, it soon became apparent that the task of draining the swamp was too daunting. The company thereafter focused solely on logging, a business that proved profitable enough that commercial logging continued in the swamp until the 1970s. Before and during the Ameri-

Activities: Canoeing, kayaking, hiking, backcountry camping.

Access Points: Chesapeake, Virginia.

Entrance fees: None.

Best times of year: October and November.

Cypress needles turn red in fall (Ian Plant).

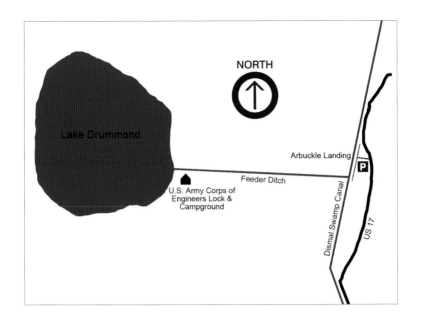

can Civil War, the swamp was a hideout for runaway slaves from the surrounding area; as many as a thousand slaves may have lived in the swamp during this time. In 1974, an Act of Congress turned Lake Drummond and the surrounding swampland into Great Dismal Swamp National Wildlife Refuge.

The lake is also steeped in myth and lore. The most popular is that of a Native American woman who died just before her wedding. Legend has it that her ghost can be seen paddling a white canoe across the waters of Lake Drummond at night. More likely, the source of strange lights at night is foxfire, a luminescence given off by burning methane escaping from decomposing vegetation or smoldering peat.

Lake Drummond is quite remote, surrounded for miles on all sides by the wilderness of the wildlife refuge. The best way to explore the lake is by canoe or kayak. It is possible you will have the entire lake to yourself, especially if you go off season or during the week. While the solitude is definitely a plus, the remote setting means that if you get into trouble you may find yourself far from help. Be especially careful!

Spring and fall are the best times to visit

Lake Drummond. Summer is popular with boaters and fisherman, making it seem a bit crowded at times; biting insects can also be a problem. The first two weeks of November are arguably the best time to paddle Lake Drummond. Crowds

Cypress trees at night (Ian Plant).

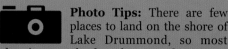

Photo Tips: There are few places to land on the shore of Lake Drummond, so most shooting must be done from your boat. Keep your camera tightly sealed within a dry bag while paddling, taking it out only when you are ready to shoot. Don't try to shoot if the water is choppy. The lake is consistently about 4-5 feet deep, even near the shore, so if using a tripod get one with tall legs, and try not to fall in!

and bugs are gone, and fall color is at its peak, with bald cypress needles turning from minty green to scarlet before dropping off the trees for winter.

Launching from Arbuckle landing, head left (south) along the Dismal Swamp Canal, part of the Atlantic Intracoastal Waterway that runs down most of the length of the Eastern Seaboard. A number of large boats use this waterway, so be careful. Head south for a little over a quarter mile; you will see a canal coming in from the right. This is the Feeder Ditch, which will lead you three miles straight to Lake Drummond. About a quarter mile before reaching the lake, you will arrive at the Lake Drummond Reservation, which is a lock maintained by the U.S. Army Corps of Engineers. When you see the lock, proceed up the left-side channel. Going past some docks, paddle to a small landing at the end of the channel near the tracks of the "boat train," a device for ferrying boats around the lock. Once on shore, carry your boat 50 feet to launch above the lock.

The U.S. Army Corps of Engineers maintains an informal camping area here, complete with bathrooms with flush toilets, grills, trash cans, non-potable water (you'll have to bring drinking water with you), an emergency phone, screened-in porches, lights, and picnic tables. During certain times of the day, maintenance staff may be on the grounds and can provide assistance in case of an emergency. Camping is prohibited elsewhere on the lake and within the surrounding swamp.

After returning to the Feeder Ditch, it is only a short distance before you enter Lake Drummond. After an hour or so of paddling beneath a closed canopy, the change in scenery is sudden and dramatic. The view opens up, with bald cypress rising from the water's surface, draped in Spanish moss. While the best cypress trees are clustered near the entrance to the Feeder Ditch, by all means explore around the edge of the lake to your heart's content. If the wind is up, the lake can get quite choppy and may be tricky for canoes or for inexperienced kayakers, so use your best judgment before heading out to open water. There are few places to land, as the shore is steep and heavily overgrown.

Unfortunately, at some point you must head back. The entrance to the Feeder Ditch is marked by an arrow sign, but is otherwise inconspicuous, so take care not to miss it, especially if you are paddling at night looking for ghost canoes. Once you find it, however, the way back is obvious. That is, if you want to leave paradise.

Total paddling distance: *The round trip from Aurbuckle Landing to the lake is about eight miles; trips across or around the lake can greatly expand the mileage and time required to complete.*

Total paddling time: *6-8 hours.*

Paddling conditions: *Flat water; high winds and choppy conditions possible.*

Directions to boat launch: *Taking Route 64 past the Norfolk area, exit onto Route 17 south. Just a few miles from the North Carolina border, turn right on Ballahack Road, then take your first right on Dismal Swamp Canal Trail to the Arbuckle Landing parking area.*

Other recreational opportunities: *There are numerous hiking and biking trails throughout Great Dismal Swamp National Wildlife Refuge, including the Washington Ditch Trail, a 4.5 mile route to a viewing platform on the north end of Lake Drummond.*

Dawn clouds over Lake Drummond's tallest cypress tree (Ian Plant).

29

Trough Creek Canyon
Trough Creek State Park, Pennsylvania

Highlights: *A hike through moss-clad forest and some of the best mountain scenery that central Pennsylvania has to offer.*

Trough Creek State Park is nestled in the mountains of central Pennsylvania. The park protects a scenic gorge formed as Great Trough Creek cuts through Terrace Mountain. With rhododendron thickets, rocky cliffs, and babbling brooks, this gem of a park has a sample of the very best that Pennsylvania has to offer. There is an extensive network of trails that begin in Trough Creek State Park and radiate out into the surrounding Rothrock State Forest. The circuit hike described here allows you to see some of the Park's many highlights, including a scenic waterfall, an erosion remnant, and an ice mine! What, exactly, is an ice mine, you ask? Read on!

The trails here are at times steep, rocky, and follow along cliffs or pass through narrow ravines. Use caution, especially during wet or icy weather.

Starting at the parking area for the **Boulder Trail**, head south and cross Great Trough Creek. On the other side of the creek, turn right on the green-blazed **Rhododendron Trail**. The rosebay rhododendron that line this trail and much of

Abbott Run (Ian Plant).

the park bloom in early July. Take the trail until you cross the Rainbow Falls Bridge over Abbot Run. Rainbow Falls is below the bridge and makes a nice scenic stop. Proceed left and begin to ascend the **Abbot Run Trail** (white blazes), which crosses the stream twice.

At the top of the short Abbot Run Trail, take a right on to the **Raven Rock Trail** (yellow blazes). It takes you by Balanced Rock, a large boulder left precariously perched on the edge of a cliff. Balanced Rock is known as an "erosion remnant" and has been on top of the cliff for thousands of years. Once part of a cliff with layers of hard and soft rocks, the softer rocks below Balanced Rock eroded away, easing Balanced Rock into its current position and leaving it stranded.

At Balanced Rock, head left on the orange-blazed **Brumbaugh Trail**, which travels for 2.4 miles through spectacular forest scenery along Trough Creek Gorge. This trail ends along Old Forge Road and Terrace Mountain Trail; turn right. After a short distance you will take a side trail that crosses over Great Trough Creek on a footbridge.

After crossing the creek, you will find yourself at the parking area for the Ice Mine, which is essentially a hole in the ground where cold air gathers and ice forms, sometimes even during warmer parts of the year. And although the Ice Mine isn't nearly as exciting as it sounds—don't expect to see glistening icicles hanging like

Activities: Hiking, biking.

Access Points: Entriken, Pennsylvania.

Entrance fees: None.

Best times of year: All year.

stalactites from the ceiling—it does make for a fun stop along the way.

From the ice mine, take the red-blazed **Boulder Trail** south until you reach the juncture with the **Laurel Run Trail**. Take the green-blazed Laurel Run Trail for 1.8 miles of scenic hiking, crossing Laurel Run numerous times by way of eight rustic bridges. You will meet up again with the Boulder Trail (via a short stint on the Terrace Mountain Road), taking it left back to your car.

Total hiking distance: *Six miles.*

Total hiking time: *3-4 hours.*

Elevation gain: *1,400 feet.*

Directions to trailhead: *The park can be reached by traveling 16 miles south from Huntingdon along Route 26, then five miles east along Route 994 near the village of Entriken.*

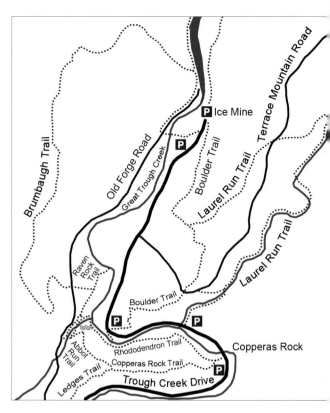

Fallen tree above Rainbow Falls (Ian Plant).

30

Pony Swim
Chincoteague National Wildlife Refuge, Virginia

Highlights: *Watch as hundreds of wild ponies are driven across the Chincoteague channel in front of 50,000 cheering spectators!*

This is the kind of adventure you might recommend only to your best friend or worst enemy. As thrilling as it is to witness hundreds of stampeding horses plunge into the water and swim several hundred feet to a far shore filled with tens of thousands of cheering spectators, it's the *waiting* for hours in the hot sun to witness this short-lived event that can drive one crazy. And all the time, you will be surrounded by drunk powerboaters and harassed by authorities if you should stray into the wrong area. Is it worth all the effort? Maybe not. But it is a unique way to witness one of the most popular outdoor events in the Mid-Atlantic area!

The Chincoteague Pony Swim and Auction take place on the last consecutive Wednesday and Thursday in the month of July. The world famous ponies are from the Virginia herd on Assateague Island, which are allowed to roam wild all year, but are actually owned by the town of Chincoteauge Volunteer Fire Department. The "Salt Water Cowboys" herd the horses across the narrowest part of Assateague Channel at low tide, after which they are herded through town and some are sold the next day at auction. The proceeds from the auction support the Fire Deparment. All remaining horses are then returned to Assateague Island, where they can roam free again.

A kayak or canoe allows one to get much closer to the ponies and away from most of the crowds. Nonetheless, several things make this trip challenging and possibly unpleasant. Part of the challenge is that you have to get to the event location early—and then wait. The exact time of the swim isn't announced until the day before the event, and often it is like waiting for the cable repairman: "sometime between 10am and 2pm . . ." Check the event website ahead of time to get an up-to-date schedule before you leave

Ponies entering the water (Ian Plant).

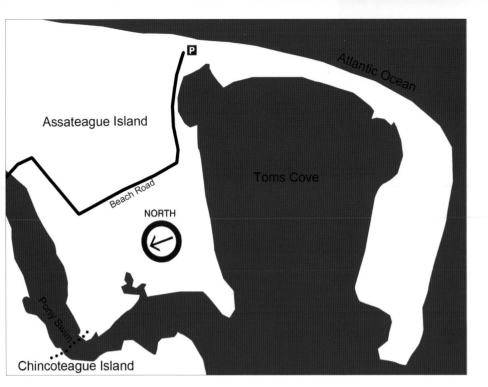

(www.chincoteague.com/pony). And since it is July, it will likely be very hot and humid! Bring a large hat to shade your head and *plenty* of sunscreen. The most challenging and dangerous aspect of this trip is that you will be surrounded by hundreds of large boats. Everyone is moving slowly, and the Coast Guard is on hand to keep things organized and safe, but still be very careful as you paddle through the fleet of pony watchers.

Launch your boat into the protected waters of Toms Cove. Head west along the cove's northern shore until you reach the channel separating Assateague Island from the town of Chincoteague. Head north into the channel. At this point you will start to encounter boats of all shapes and sizes. Within less than 1.5 miles you will arrive, unmistakably, at your destination (the hundreds of boats and thousands of people all gathered at the same place should probably clue you in). The Coast Guard cordons off a path for the ponies to swim, and boats are allowed to weigh anchor on either side of the path. By the way, obey ALL instructions that the Coast Guard may give you. There is

typically a spot near the shore where kayakers and canoeists gather. Take up position, and wait for the fun to begin!

Total paddling distance: *Approximately seven miles out and back.*

Total paddling time: *3-5 hours.*

Paddling conditions: *Flat water, but you will encounter many powerboats.*

Directions to boat launch: *From the town of Chincoteague, enter the National Wildlife Refuge and take Beach Road all the way to the end; turn right into the parking area and find a spot with easy access to the waters of Toms Cove.*

Activities: Kayaking, canoeing.

Access Points: Chincoteague, Virginia.

Entrance fees: $5 per vehicle.

Best times of year: The last Wednesday of every July.

31

Wildflowers and Rock Art
Holtwood Preserve, Pennsylvania

Highlights: *One of the Mid-Atlantic's most incredible wildflowers displays, along with a bonus paddle to native American petroglyphs!*

The Holtwood Environmental Preserve in Lancaster County, Pennsylvania is a good example of how corporations can act to preserve the environment. Owned and operated by PPL Corporation, the 5,000 acre preserve successfully combines out-door recreation and environmental pro-tection with hydroelectric power genera-tion. It is a very good thing, too, because the preserve contains two incredible trea-sures: one of the best wildflower displays in the Mid-Atlantic area, as well as one of the best examples of native American petroglyphs found in the Eastern United States.

To see the wildflowers, visit Shenk's Ferry Wildlflower Preserve. Toward the end of April the preserve comes alive with acres of erect white trillium and wild blue phlox, along with a host of other species. Easy trails wind through the preserve along Grubb Run. A number of species bloom throughout the rest of spring and summer, but late April is when the flower display is most intense.

After you've had your fill of wildflowers, it's time to visit the famous Safe Harbor petroglyphs. Just hop in your canoe or kayak and head upriver! You did bring your canoe or kayak, right? Well, in any

Activities: Hiking, paddling.

Access Points: Pequea, Pennsylvania.

Entrance fees: None.

Best times of year: Late April.

event, the petroglyphs are located on is-lands in the middle of the Susquehanna River, just below Safe Harbor Dam. The best way to reach the glyphs is to launch from the public boat ramp in the nearby

White erect trillium (Ian Plant).

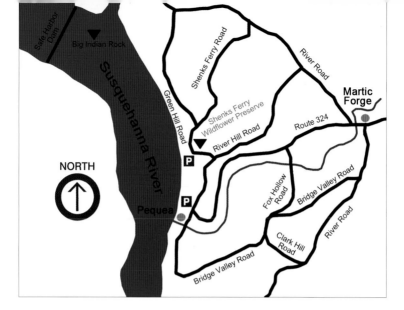

town of Pequea. Paddle upstream for about two miles until you start to see a bunch of rock islands right below the dam. Look for one big rock sticking out of the water by itself, taller than any other rock you see. This will be Big Indian Rock, which has the best petroglyphs (along with a number of more recently carved rock art, otherwise known as grafitti). Carefully moor your boat, as the current can get fairly strong on the river just below the dam and scheduled releases may cause the water level to rise rapidly. Climb to the top to see the carved figures of bird men, lizard dogs, and other strange creatures. Anthropologists believe that the carvings may have been used to denote seasons and favorite fish-

ing and hunting spots. Or maybe the carvers were just bored!

Total distance: *1-3 miles hiking (wildflower preserve); 4-5 miles paddling (petroglyphs).*

Total time: *1-2 miles hiking (wildflowers); 2-3 hours paddling (petroglyphs).*

Paddling conditions: *Flat water with a current that gets stronger as you approach the dam, subject to high winds.*

Directions to wildflower trailhead: *From Route 272 (Lancaster Pike) in Lancaster County, take Route 324 west to Martic Ford. Turn right on River Road; travel for several miles before turning left on Shenks Ferry Road. Shenks Ferry Road leads to Green Hill Road; take another left to reach the wildflower preserve. Green Hill Road is a dirt road that gets rough in a few places, but is usually easily driven by cars.*

Directions to Pequea boat launch: *From the wildlflower preserve continue on Green Hill Road until you hit River Hill Road. Take a right and in a short while you will be in Pequea. The boat launch is hard to miss.*

Native American petroglyphs (Ian Plant).

32

Lostland Run Loop
Potomac State Forest, Maryland

Highlights: *A scenic hike through a wild forest with great views of cascading streams and the Potomac River.*

Nestled in the rugged mountains of Western Maryland lies the Potomac State Forest, with 11,000 acres of untamed forest and trout-filled streams bordering a beautiful stretch of the North Fork of the Potomac River. Potomac State Forest is where the outdoor enthusiast's dreams come true. The great diversity of meadows, streams and dense woods supports a large variety of wildlife including fox, black bears, wild turkeys, whitetail deer and numerous song birds. Along with the diversity of wildlife comes an even greater array of flora. The woods are a densely forested canopy of hardwood deciduous trees, and its wild streams and rivers drain the mountains into the mighty Potomac River.

There are many miles of dirt roads that pierce the Potomac State forest, but there is really only one way to truly appreciate its beauty and wildness: you must get out of the car and take a long walk into the woods. The very best trail in the area is

Activities: Hiking.

Access Points: Oakland, Maryland.

Entrance fees: None.

Best times of year: April through October.

the **Lostland Run Trail**. This rugged loop hike passes through primeval woods, over rough rock-strewn paths, alongside the tumbling waters of Lostland Run to a beautiful waterfall known as Cascade Falls, and finally down to the bottom of a hollow to a scenic vista overlooking the Potomac River.

Start the hike by parking your car at the Forest Headquarters off of Potomac Camp Road. Walk across the road back up to a wooden marker and the beginning of the hike. The path enters the woods

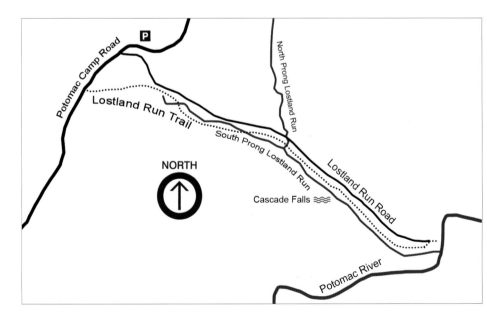

and you will be hiking downhill for the entire length of the first section of the loop hike. You cross several footbridges over Lostland Run along the way. At three miles, you will reach the rush and tumble of Cascade Falls. A viewing platform offers a great vista of the waterfall, and you will most likely want to spend some time exploring its environs and taking in the beauty and tranquility of the scene.

After leaving the falls, the trail enters into its most solitary section of the hike. Alternating between climbing along steep bluffs and walking along the stream, you will make your way towards the small dirt parking lot for the Potomac River Overlook. Take a quick hike up the small path to the steep cliffs of the overlook for a wonderful vista of the Potomac River and the wilderness of the Potomac State Forest. Hike up the dirt **Lostland Run Road** back to your car.

Total distance: 7.4 mile loop.

Total time: 4-5 hours.

Elevation gain: 650 feet.

Directions to trailhead: Follow Route 70 west to Route 68 west. Continue on Route 68 to exit 14 (Route 219). Follow Route 219 south to Oakland. Continue straight at the traffic light (Route 135 east). Travel 1 mile to the intersection of Route 560. At the traffic light, turn right onto Route 560 south and travel 3 miles to Bethlehem Road. Turn left on Bethlehem Road and travel 2 miles to the intersection of Bethlehem Road and Eagle Rock Road. Turn right, staying on Bethlehem Road for 1.4 miles. Turn left on Combination Road and travel 0.5 miles. Turn left on Potomac Camp Road and travel 0.5 miles to the Forest Resource Center, which will be on the left.

Cascade Falls on Lostland Run (Joseph Rossbach).

33

Swallow Falls
Swallow Falls State Park, Maryland

Highlights: *Several majestic waterfalls, including Maryland's tallest, along the wild and extremely scenic Youghiogheny River.*

Swallow Falls State Park is a little known gem to the residents of Maryland, let alone the Mid-Atlantic at large. Packed into this small 257 acre park are tons of great scenery, old growth hemlock forests, the wild and mighty Youghiogheny River and Maryland's tallest waterfall, Muddy Creek Falls. This park has a little bit of everything for everyone, from a great hike along the Yough and Muddy Creek, to kayaking on the river and family camping.

The Youghiogheny River flows along the park's borders, passing house-sized boulders and rocky gorges, creating rapids and dropping powerfully at Swallow Falls. For the adventurous white water lover, a kayak or rafting run down the Yough offers a first class experience that is hard to beat in the Mid-Atlantic (local guide services are available for those without the skills to do it themselves).

Upper Swallow Falls (Joseph Rossbach).

For the less adventurous traveler, there is a wonderful loop hike through the park that will take you through an ancient stand of old growth hemlock woods, past Muddy Creek Falls, and along the banks of the Youghiogheny River up to Swallow and Tolliver Falls.

Start the hike at the first parking lot, just left of the entrance gate; hit the trailhead and you will immediately be transferred back in time as you travel through a hauntingly beautiful old growth hemlock forest. Continue to follow the trail until you reach a small boardwalk that leads to a ledge overlooking Maryland's tallest waterfall, Muddy Creek Falls. You can continue down a set of steps to the base of the falls, which will often completely freeze over in the winter and form a cascading series of giant icicles. Continue to follow the trail along Muddy Creek for a short distance, and then you will come to the steep and scenic banks of the Youghiogheny. From here you will hike among hemlock and hardwood forests, with large boulders littering the sides of the trail.

As you continue to follow the trail you will eventually come to the base of Swallow Falls, where you might be treated with the sight of kayakers braving the rapid waters and dropping through the spouts and down river. Sit down and soak up the view and listen to the thundering falls for a while, before continuing along the trail to Tolliver Run and a small and pristine waterfall. From here you will travel through

Activities: Hiking.

Access Points: Herrington Manor, Maryland.

Entrance fees: Memorial Day-Labor Day $3/person; Labor Day-Memorial Day $2/vehicle. Out-of-state residents add $1 to all day use service charges.

Best times of year: Spring through autumn.

Lower Swallow Falls (Ian Plant).

he woods past towering trees
back to the parking lot.

Total hiking distance: *One
mile round trip.*

Total hiking time: *One-half
hour; more if you explore.*

Elevation gain: *Negligible.*

Directions to trailhead:
*Follow Route 68 west to exit
14; take Route 219 south 19.5
miles to Mayhew Inn Road.
Turn right on Mayhew Inn
Road, travel 4.5 miles to the
end and turn left on to Oakland Sang Run Road. Travel
0.3 miles and turn right on to
Swallow Falls Road, which
leads to the park.*

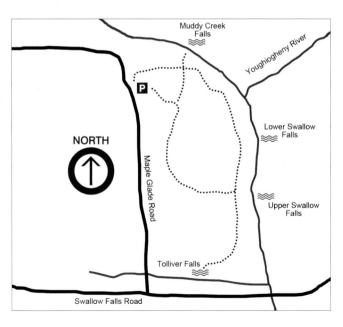

34

Blackwater Canyon
Blackwater Falls State Park, West Virginia

Highlights: *One of the most dramatic canyons and dramatic waterfalls in the Mid-Atlantic area, and one of the best places to see fall color—anywhere!*

Blackwater Canyon is a steep and rugged eight-mile long gorge carved out by the Blackwater River in the Allegheny Mountains of eastern West Virginia. The canyon is located adjacent to and inside of Blackwater Falls State Park, so named for the magnificent and thundering waterfall that drops 62 feet from its peaceful and rolling course in Canaan Valley. This waterfall is so beautiful and popular that thousands of tourists flock here each year just to catch a glimpse of the falls. What most of them miss is one of the most rugged and beautiful canyons in the eastern United States.

There are many ways to explore the canyon, and there are a lot of hikes and other adventures to be found here. The first thing you should do when visiting the park is to take the short hike down to the park's namesake: Blackwater Falls. This thundering cascade drops over a sheer ledge into the canyon below. To reach Blackwater Falls, enter the park and head to the visitor center and gift shop. Park and follow the wooden boardwalk down to a viewing platform that puts you at eye level with the falls.

Blackwater Falls isn't the only waterfall in the park—there are numerous other falls that, although lacking in Blackwater's size and power, are no less beautiful. A particularly scenic set of falls can be found along Shay Run. From the Blackwater Falls Lodge parking lot, look for the trail to the left of the lodge near the indoor pool, leading into the woods. This is the **Elakala Trail**. Follow the trail for less than 0.5 miles until you reach a footbridge and Elakala Falls directly below.

For the adventurous types, head over the footbridge and follow a small steep path to the right down to the base of the falls. From here, spend time enjoying the falls as it drops over emerald moss-covered rocks into the chasm. You can continue to follow Shay Run as it makes its steep descent into Blackwater Canyon, passing several scenic falls along the way. Please note that at this point you are not on a trail, and are simply following the course of the stream. It can be very slippery and dangerous, and should not be attempted by those in poor physical condition or with disabilities. That being said, this is an adventurous scramble around house-sized boulders and along many more wonderful waterfalls.

Activities: Hiking.

Access Points: Davis, West Virginia.

Entrance fees: None.

Best times of year: Anytime of year is a great time to visit Blackwater Canyon, but early October during peak fall color may be the very best!

Above: Elakala Falls (Joseph Rossbach). Right: Blackwater Canyon (Ian Plant)

Shay Run in autumn (Joseph Rossbach)

Once you've had your fill of Shay Run, return to the Elakala Trail and continue along until you pass the park road. Crossing the road, the trail becomes the **Balanced Rock Trail**. Follow the trail to the intersection with the **Red Spruce Riding Trail**. At this point you can continue on for another half-mile to Balanced Rock, a large boulder on a rock

ledge with nice views. Then back track your steps to the junction with the Red Spruce Riding Trail and turn right.

The trail now follows an old road grade that is moss-covered and often very muddy. Continue on until you reach the **Davis Trail** a short time after crossing Engine Run, a small stream. Turn left on

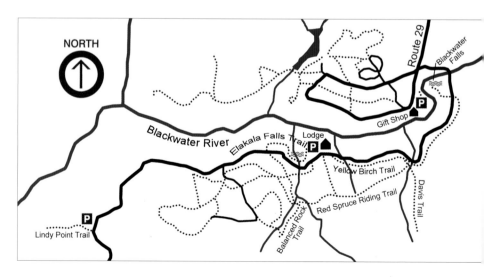

the Davis Trail, and follow it to the junction with the **Yellow Birch Trail**. Follow the Yellow Birch Trail through the dark and mysterious forest of yellow birch and spruce back to the parking lot and your car at the lodge.

Want more? Hop back in your car and continue past the lodge until the road becomes the **Canaan Loop Road**, an unimproved dirt road. Before the road becomes a full-on 4x4 trail, there is a parking area for the **Lindy Point Trail**, which heads 0.3 miles to Lindy Point Overlook, a dramatic spot perched atop rugged cliffs. Still not enough? There are plenty of trails to be found in the park and surrounding areas!

Total hiking distance: *Over five miles for all of the trails described.*

Total hiking time: *4-5 hours.*

Elevation gain: *Several hundred feet.*

Directions to trailhead: *From Route 32, head to the town of Davis. When in town, take Route 29 into the park.*

Not had enough of Blackwater Canyon? Don't fret, there's plenty more adventure to be found. Another great hike is the **Canyon Rim Trail**, which starts from a trailhead off of Forest Road 717 and heads 2.4 miles one-way to several jaw-dropping overlooks of the canyon. To reach the trailhead, take a left on Route 219 in the town of Thomas and follow it for 6.5 miles to forest road 18. Turn left on Forest Road 18, and follow it for one-half mile to Forest Road 717. Follow Forest Road 717 for 1.2 miles; the Canyon Rim Trail will be on your left.

Looking to stretch your leg muscles in a different way? Consider biking the Blackwater Canyon Trail, an old railroad grade that runs for ten miles alongside the Blackwater River between the towns of Thomas and Hendricks. The trail drops 1,300 feet at is passes unique cut-stone arches, waterfalls, and scenic rapids. The eastern trailhead can be reached from the town of Thomas off of Douglas Road. The western trailhead can be reached in the town of Hendricks off of Second Street.

Blackwater Falls in winter (Joseph Rossbach).

North Fork Mountain
Monongahela National Forest, West Virginia

Highlights: *Miles and miles of sandstone cliffs and views to die for on West Virginia's premiere mountain trail.*

Heralded as the best hike in West Virginia, North Fork Mountain's rocky cliffs soar above the Potomac River Valley. From the exposed ridge of the mountain, the adventurous hiker is rewarded with tremendous panoramic views of the surrounding forest as well as Seneca Rocks, Dolly Sods, Champe Rocks, Germany Valley and Hopeville Gorge. Simply put, this is an incredible hike!

North Fork Mountain can be hiked in sections, but if you are really feeling up for a one-of-a-kind wilderness experience, hike the entire 24 miles of the superlative **North Fork Mountain Trail**. Unless you are in extremely good condition, it is best to do this hike as an overnight backpack. Not only will you be able to slow down a bit and really appreciate the beautiful mountain scenery, you also have a chance to spend a night under the stars. Some of the clearest skies in the east lie in West Virginia, and lying on the ground at night staring into the heavens on top of a wild and lonely mountain ridge is something you must experience in your lifetime. A note of caution: this trail is dry—*bone* dry! You will need to carry all of your drinking water with you, as there are no springs or streams.

Start from the southern end; the elevation gain is less heading south to north. The trail is very easy to follow and is marked with blue blazes. Along the way you will often be treated with great views, as the trail follows the crest of the mountain. There are many great informal camping spots along the trail.

There are several parking areas that you will cross during the hike. These areas can make convenient places to cache water, food, and other supplies, or they can serve as end-points of shorter hikes.

If you don't feel up to the challenge of hiking all of North Fork Mountain, consider hiking from the northern trailhead to Chimney Top, the most dramatic spot along the entire trail. Chimney Top affords spectacular views to the north and west, and is a landscape photographer's dream. The trail to Chimney Rocks is 2.5 miles long and ascends over 1,750.

Total hiking distance: *24 miles one way.*

Total hiking time: *Two days.*

Elevation gain: *Plenty of significant ups and down.*

Directions to northern trailhead: *From Petersburg, take Route 28/55 south. Turn right on CR28/11 (Smoke Hole Road). Look for a sign for Big Bend at the intersection. Cross the bridge over the river and go 0.5 miles to the small parking area on the right.*

Activities: Hiking, backcountry camping.

Access Points: Petersburg, West Virginia.

Entrance fees: None.

Best times of year: May through early October.

Directions to southern trailhead: *At the intersection of Route 220 and Route 33 in Franklin, take Route 220 north/Route 33 west 0.5 mile and make a left onto Route 33 west. Go 8.2 miles to the top of North Fork Mountain. Parking is on the right. There is a small metal building and gate across the road from the parking lot; this is private land. Do not block the gate or you may be towed!*

North Fork Mountain (Ian Plant).

Hiking North Fork Mountain; self portrait (Joseph Rossbach).

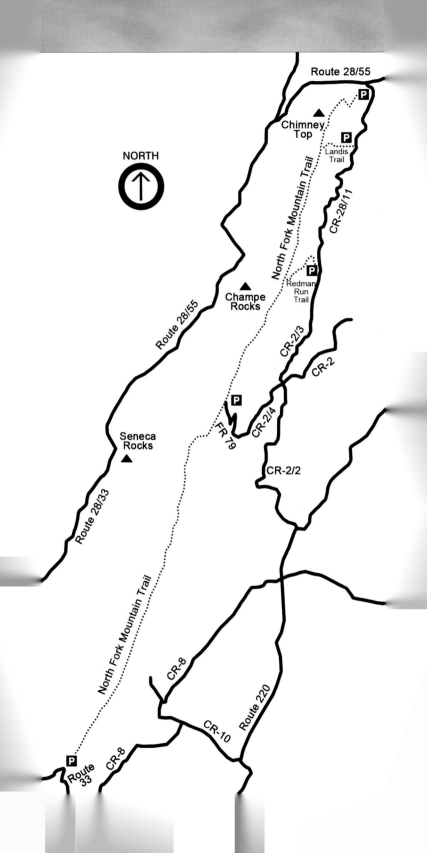

Seneca Rocks
Monongahela National Forest,
West Virginia

Highlights: *A moderate hike to the top of a precarious perch with a stunning 900 foot drop!*

(Joseph Rossbach)

Towering above the North Fork South Branch of the Potomac River, Seneca Rocks abruptly rise nearly 900 vertical feet from the valley below. The razorback and rigid fins of Seneca Rocks are of the Limestone/Tuscarora formation, and can be seen for miles from Route 28 on the drive in to the small, but scenic, hamlet of Seneca Rocks.

Seneca Rocks, and nearby Champe Rocks, are two of the most impressive natural land forms in the state. Geologically speaking, the Seneca Rocks formation is a Tuscarora quartzite that was laid down around 440 million years ago, as thick sand deposits on the edge of an ancient and long forgotten ocean. Eons of geologic activity, heat, and pressure formed the almost 250 foot thick limestone deposits. Over the course of millions of years of uplift and erosion, Seneca Rocks and the many crags and precipices of the surrounding mountain tops have taken on their current appearance.

Exploring this geologic phenomenon is a great way to spend the weekend in the wild mountains of West Virginia. From the Seneca Rocks Discovery Center, you get an impressive view of the towering precipice and its rough crags. The Discovery Center is also a great place to start out your day. Inside you will find answers to your questions of how this impressive formation came to be, as well as interpre-

tive programs on most weekends, and information on local wildlife and pioneer history of the surrounding Appalachian mountain area.

Rock climbing is by far the most popular outdoor adventure at Seneca Rocks, and with over 16 well established climbing routes—with colorful names like Break Neck, the Tomato, West Pole, Crispy Critter and Neck Press to name a few—it holds some of the most challenging pitches in the Mid-Atlantic. There are several great outfitters in town that can get you geared up and guide you up the wall, if you are up to the challenge!

For those who want to experience the thrill of standing atop the rocks but are not ready to strap on a harness and pitch a route up the vertical walls, there is a short but steep hike that will deliver you to the top, with a 360 degree view of the surrounding mountains, including Spruce Knob, North Fork Mountain and Dolly Sods to the north.

Leaving the picnic parking area, cross a well built and beautiful foot bridge that spans the North Fork South Branch Potomac River. From here, it's a near vertical climb for the next mile up the steep hill-

Activities: Hiking, rock climbing.

Access Points: Seneca Rocks, West Virginia.

Entrance fees: None.

Best times of year: Spring through autumn.

Below Seneca Rocks (Ian Plant).

side to the top and the viewing platform. This is a particularly nice place to spend a sunset, watching the light paint the top of the rocks and cast its long shadows across the valley below. You can scramble up the rocks to the very top, but please keep in mind that the terrain is steep, rugged and unforgiving. We do not recommend venturing out along the knife edge summit without proper climbing gear and proper skills (or a guide).

Total hiking distance: *2.6 miles round trip.*

Total hiking time: *2-3 hours.*

Elevation gain: *900 feet.*

Directions to trailhead: *About 0.2 miles north of the juncture of Route 33 and Route 28/55, turn into the Seneca Rocks picnic area parking lot.*

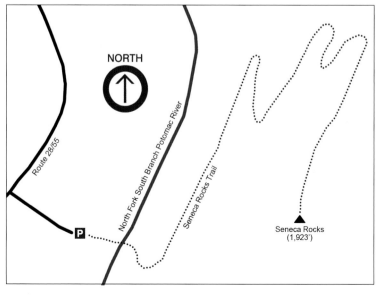

Bear Rocks
Bear Rocks Preserve,
Dolly Sods, West Virginia

Highlights: *A short hike through a slice of arctic tundra to interesting rock formations and great mountain views.*

Located on a high and lonely plateau in the Allegheny Mountains of eastern West Virginia is one of the Mid-Atlantic's most remarkable and stunning natural areas. Here, one will find windswept plains, upland bogs, rock outcrops and wide open vistas, surrounded by the rolling mountains and hardwood forests of the Alleghenies. The terrain looks like something out of the arctic tundra—it is hard to believe that you are not in Alaska, but rather south of the Mason-Dixon line!

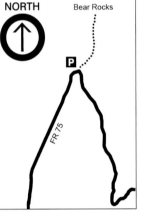

The wild lands of the Allegheny Front were often avoided by early settlers in the East. As one noted columnist of 1852 once wrote, "...entirely uninhabited, and so savage and inaccessible that it has rarely been penetrated, even by the most adventurous." Nowadays, even the less adventurous can penetrate this wild landscape, but it still beckons the most adventurous as well.

The name Dolly Sods derives from the name Dahle, a German family who farmed and grazed the land. The resulting open field were known as "sods." During World War II, Dolly Sods was used as a bombing range. Although most of the ordinance has been accounted for, on occasion people do find shells, and although extremely rare, sometimes even live ordinance. So step carefully!

Your patience will be tested as you leave the smooth highway and enter into the forest traveling along the winding and often bumpy graded dirt road of FR 75. The five mile drive leads you through a hardwood forest with limited views of the

surrounding mountains under a canopy of lush foliage, and is sure to jar the senses bump after bump as you ascend 2,000 vertical feet toward the lonely windswept plateau above. As you make your way towards the top, the forest all of a sudden gives way to huge outcrops of rocks, and in the last 100 yards of the drive, opens up with 360-degree vistas of the Allegheny Mountains and the Bear Rocks Preserve. You are 4,000 feet above sea level on an open plateau, and the views are incredible!

Bear Rocks Preserve is not an area of difficult hiking, but rather a location for exploration and rock scrambling along the ridges and open tundra, filled with blueberries and stunted red spruce trees that lean toward the east from the relentless winds that sweep across the open expanse. From the parking lot, there are many small trails that lead you out to the rocks. Upon reaching the rocks at the edge of the mountain ridge, you get a great view to the southeast, with North Fork Mountain and its striking curved cliffs winding off

Activities: Hiking, backpacking.

Access Points: Petersburg, West Virginia.

Entrance fees: None.

Best times of year: Late September through early October. Dolly Sods' roads are closed in winter.

Dolly Sods in autumn (Joseph Rossbach).

into the distance. Simply hike along the rocks and explore all of the amazing formations. You can continue for about 0.5 to 0.75 miles along the rocks with amazing vistas in all directions. Be sure to wear a sturdy pair of hiking boots, as you will be rock hopping and scrambling along steep cliffs with a drop of over fifty feet.

Looking to stretch your legs a bit more? You have open terrain to the north, west, and south. Explore to your heart's content! Either hike across country, or take one of many paths that carve through the Dolly Sods Wilderness. Just don't get lost—a good compass is useful in this regard. Also, be aware that there are a number of boggy areas, so if things start to get soggy, change course and search for firmer terrain.

The weather at Bear Rocks can change in an instant, and you should be prepared for the possibility of cold conditions and even sleet and snow all times of year—even in the summer!

Total hiking distance: 0.75 miles round trip; more if you explore the open country around you.

Total hiking time: One-half hour; more if you explore.

Elevation gain: Negligible.

Directions to trailhead: Take Route 55 west to Jordan Run Road (Route 28/7). Take Jordan Run Road for several miles, then turn left onto FR 75. Continue on FR 75 to the top of the plateau. Where the road veers sharply to the left, you will find the Bear Rocks parking lot. Note that the Forest Service roads are not open in winter, making auto access impossible. For a true winter wilderness experience, one can hike, snowshoe, or cross-country ski up the closed road.

Rohrbaugh Plains
Dolly Sods, West Virginia

Highlights: *An epic journey through some of the best alpine scenery in the Mid-Atlantic area.*

This hike travels through some of the best scenery that Dolly Sods has to offer. You will pass through hardwood and evergreen forests, arrive at a huge rock outcropping with majestic views down Red Creek Canyon, pass through open wildflower-choked meadows, ford the cold waters of Red Creek, traverse wetland bogs, and see rhododendron and fern-filled woodlands—sounds good, eh?

This shuttle hike can be done in a long day or as an overnight backpack. Hikers should bring a sturdy pair of hiking boots and cold weather gear appropriate for the season. Remember that because of the high elevation, temperatures can sometimes fall below freezing here even in the summer, and thunderstorms are a common occurrence in these rugged mountains.

Start the hike on the **Rohrbaugh Plains Trail** at the Dolly Sods Picnic Area by crossing the forest road. Look for a narrow footpath into the woods. You will see a kiosk within a couple of yards; be sure to sign in. The first part of this hike leads through a beautiful forest, littered with ferns on the forest floor and many small stream crossings. There are quite a few small game trails that intersect with the trail, but it is easy to follow the main path. After hiking for 1.5 miles, you will come to a huge rock outcrop with stunning views down Red Creek Canyon. There is a great campsite nestled in a thicket of rhododendron just off the trail, and there is a small spring for filtering water just a little further north on the trail.

From here the small footpath turns into an old forest road, and travels for 0.75

Red Creek (Joseph Rossbach).

miles to the junction with the Wildlife Trail. The Rohrbaugh Plains Trail will take off sharply to the left at the junction, and turns into a rough and rocky railroad grade for 0.4 miles to the junction with the **Fisher Springs Trail**. Fisher Springs is a beautiful little stream, and is choked with lichen-covered boulders and small waterfalls. You will want to go straight (to the left) and follow the Fisher Springs Trail for one mile until you reach Red Creek. Just before reaching Red Creek, there is a small trail that takes off to the right and follows the creek to some amazing backcountry campsites. After 0.25 miles, you will arrive at a thundering waterfall with a huge plunge pool, perfect for an afternoon lunch and a dip in the refreshing and cool waters of the creek.

After lunch and a dip, return to the main trail and ford Red Creek. The water can be ankle deep in the summer and up to waist deep in the spring or after a hard rain. A trekking pole will help you navigate across the ford. After fording the creek take the **Red Creek Trail** north, trudging uphill along a steep trail that turns into a railroad grade after 0.5 miles. In about two

Activities: Hiking, backpacking.

Access Points: Petersburg, West Virginia.

Entrance fees: None.

Best times of year: Spring through autumn.

miles you reach the Forks of Red Creek. The waterfalls, swimming holes, and all around spectacular scenery will beckon you to explore the area and bask in its beauty. When you've had your fill, cross the left fork of Red Creek and follow the trail through the woods, climbing to an open meadow with the views and scenery that Dolly Sods is famous for.

At the end of the meadow, enter into the woods once again and after 0.9 miles from the Forks, you will arrive at the junction with the **Blackbird Knob Trail**. Turn right, and follow the Blackbird Knob Trail across tundra plains of blueberry and wild azalea, an ecosystem more reminiscent of the Canadian tundra than that of the Mid-Atlantic Appalachian mountains. Keep in mind that you will be hiking through areas of thick mud that are nearly impossible to avoid. Towards the end of the trail you will encounter a boardwalk. At this point you are but a short distance from the end of the trail and your shuttle vehicle.

Total hiking distance: 10 miles.

Total hiking time: 6-7 hours.

Elevation gain: 1,200 feet.

Directions to trailhead: From Route 28/55, turn right on to Jordan Run Road. In 0.9 miles, pass the first turn off to Dolly Sods on the left, FR 19. In 6.7 more miles, turn left onto FR 75 (marked with signs for Dolly Sods). FR 75 soon becomes a gravel road. It is graded, but still has some rather bumpy parts. As you reach the top of the mountain, the large trees will disappear and the road will make a final sharp left-hand turn. Travel another 2.4 miles to the Blackbird Knob Trail parking area, which is marked with a kiosk (if you come to the Red Creek Campground you went to far). Leave a vehicle, and continue south on FR 75. In 5.1 miles, come to an intersection with FR 19; bear right and drive to the Dolly Sods Picnic Area on the left.

Ferns in autumn (Joseph Rossbach).

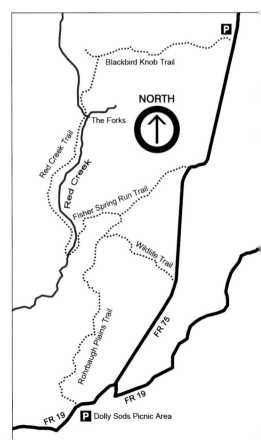

View of Red Creek Canyon (Joseph Rossbach).

Crabtree Falls
George Washington National Forest, Virginia

Highlights: *A cascading series of waterfalls tumbling over 1,200 feet down a steep mountainside.*

Cascading down 1,200 feet, Crabtree Falls holds the title as the tallest waterfall in the United States east of the Mississippi River. Of course, many waterfalls *claim* that title, and indeed, many single-drop waterfalls in the east are taller than any of the individual drops that make up the series of cascades that are collectively called Crabtree Falls. But who are we to argue? Located in the George Washington National Forest just off the Blue Ridge Parkway, Crabtree Falls is a day hiker's paradise. With five major vertical drops, the largest being a tumbling cascade 400 feet high, thousands of gallons of water spill over the falls and beckon the adventurer to explore.

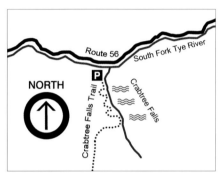

Crabtree Falls offers serenity and isolation in a forest stream setting that is beautiful in all four seasons. Summer is the most heavily visited time of the year; but it can also be the least scenic, with water levels often low from lack of precipitation. Autumn and spring are the best times to visit. In the spring, the water furiously pounds down the cascades, and the woods are alive with wildflowers and wildlife. In the fall, the trees come to life in a kaleidoscope of color from red to purple. Winter can be a truly magical time to visit the falls, with interesting ice formations and snow covered trees.

The first falls overlook, located only a few hundred feet from the parking lot, offers access to all visitors with a gentle paved trail. But don't make this your only stop! There is plenty more for you to see, and the scenery gets progressively better the higher you climb.

For the more adventurous hiker, you may continue up the trail to the top of the upper falls, passing four more waterfall overlooks along the way. The top of the upper falls offers great views of the spectacular Tye River Valley and surrounding mountains, and makes the perfect place for lunch. At this point you can retrace your steps back to the parking area, or continue to explore more; after the upper falls, the trail continues up towards Crabtree Meadows and the Appalachian Trail.

Total hiking distance: *3.6 miles round trip to upper falls.*

Total hiking time: *2-3 hours.*

Elevation gain: *1,300 feet.*

Directions to trailhead: *The parking area is off of Route 56, which can be accessed either to the north from the Blue Ridge Parkway, or from the south from Route 29 just south of Lovingston.*

Activities: Hiking.

Access Points: Lovingston, Virginia.

Entrance fees: $3 per vehicle per day.

Best times of year: Any.

One of Crabtree's many falls (Joseph Rossbach).

Blue Ridge Traverse
Mt. Pleasant National Scenic Area, Virginia

Highlights: *A moderately challenging hike that passes several grand scenic views of the Blue Ridge Mountains.*

Fantastic scenic views of the majestic Blue Ridge Mountains, gently sloping mountain trails, a jaunt on the Appalachian Trail over an open bald—who could ask for anything more? The Mount Pleasant Scenic Area in central Virginia, created by an Act of Congress in 1994, protects a particularly scenic (hence the name) swath of the George Washington National Forest. The hike described here takes you on a pleasant (once again,

Trail to reach the summit in 0.5 miles. Upon reaching the summit ridge, you have the choice of going left or right for two different views: one east and one west. Both viewpoints are excellent. There are a number of nice campsites on the summit ridge, making it a perfect place to stay if you want to photograph sunset or sunrise, but bring plenty of water with you as there are no water sources on the rocky summit.

Autumn view from summit of Mt. Pleasant (Ian Plant).

Views from either point are stunning. Looking east, one sees rolling farmland; looking north, west, or south, the Blue Ridge Mountains march in an endless parade to the horizon. As is often the case with this remote area, you may be lucky enough to have it all to yourself; if so, enjoy!

Backtracking to the intersection, head toward Pompey Mountain. You hike up and over the wooded summit (there are no good views), and then begin your descent, with the trail gradually widening to become an old dirt road. At 5.5 miles you are back to the parking lot.

hence the name) stroll through open forest to the summits of three 4,000 foot peaks, two of which have stunning mountain views. You even have a short stint on the Appalachian Trail, which stretches over 2,000 miles from Georgia to Maine.

Starting at the parking area, take the **Henry Lanum Trail** toward Mount Pleasant, which starts off as an old dirt road and eventually narrows to a foot path. After a steady but moderate climb through open forest for 2.3 miles, you reach an intersection at the top of a ridge. Turn right on the **Mount Pleasant**

Activities: Hiking, backcountry camping.

Access Points: Forks of Buffalo, Virginia.

Entrance fees: None.

Best times of year: May-October.

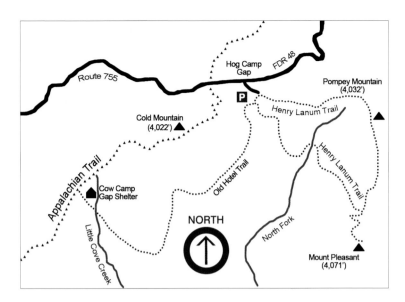

For the second part of this hike, cross the road and head up the **Old Hotel Trail** for 3.3 miles until reaching the intersection with the white-blazed **Appalachian Trail**, passing the Cow Gap Camp Shelter along the way. Turning right at the AT, not before long you will come out into the open along the summit of 4,022-foot Cold Mountain. Controlled burns and mechanical brush cutting keep the summit open, with unobstructed panoramic views in all directions. After spending some time on the open bald soaking in the views (who knows, maybe even a night or two!), eventually it will be time to leave. Descend Cold Mountain until you hit unpaved Forest Road 48, taking it back to the parking area.

Total hiking distance: *12 miles double loop round trip.*

Total hiking time: *6-8 hours.*

Elevation gain: *2,800 feet.*

Directions to trailhead: *From Route 29 South, take Route 60 west toward the Blue Ridge Parkway. After the Long Mountain Wayside, turn right on to Route 634 (keep an eye out for signs directing you to the Mt. Pleasant Scenic Area). Turn right on to Route 755, which becomes dirt FR 48. After reaching a*

parking area along the Appalachian Trail, continue 0.4 miles and turn right on FR 51 (if the gate is closed, park in the parking area and continue on foot). Take FR 51 for a few hundred feet to a small parking area at the trailhead.

Butter-and-eggs on Cold Mountain (Ian Plant).

Nearby attractions: Panther Falls and Staton's Creek Falls are two incredible waterfalls, both easily accessible from Route 60. Staton's Creek Falls, dropping 140 feet over several cascades, can be reached directly off of CR 633 (Fiddlers Green Way). The smaller and more popular Panther Falls is a short hike from FR 315 (Panther Falls Road).

Sharp Top
Blue Ridge Parkway, Virginia

Highlights: *A moderate hike to one of the best views on the Blue Ridge Parkway.*

Once thought to be Virginia's highest peak, Sharp Top Mountain, with its conical summit, offers 360 degree views of the surrounding Blue Ridge Mountains. Below the summit lies the scenic Blue Ridge Parkway, which stretches 469 miles from the southern terminus of Shenandoah National Park, running across the snaking spine of the Blue Ridge Mountains, all the way down to Great Smoky Mountains National Park in North Carolina.

Activities: Hiking.

Access Points: Peaks of Otter area, Blue Ridge Parkway, Virginia.

Entrance fees: None.

Best times of year: April through late October.

Seen from miles around, the striking and rocky 3,875 foot summit of Sharp Top Mountain is a major landmark along the Blue Ridge Parkway, and one of Virginia's premier scenic attractions. You will start the hike near mile marker 86 of the Parkway. The trail enters the woods opposite of the Peaks of Otter Visitor Center and just next to the camp store.

The hike begins with the sound of passing motorists traveling the Parkway, but it doesn't take long before the sound of rushing cars is replaced with the soft symphony of the woodland habitat. At just 0.2 miles into the hike, you will cross the bus road where shuttle buses ferry tourists near the summit in the busy season (spring through fall). After crossing the road, you re-enter the woods and continue the steep climb towards the summit of the mountain. After hiking for one mile, you will reach the first good view of the surrounding mountains. Go another 0.2

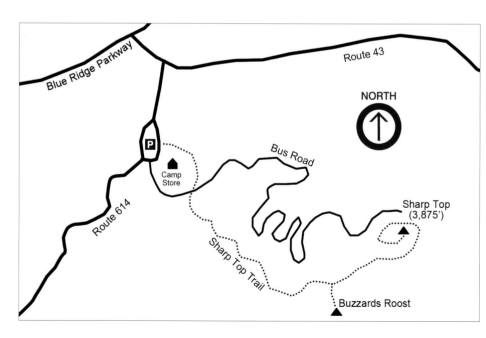

miles and there is a side trail that leads to Buzzards Roost, a great spot to have a picnic and suck in the awesome scenery.

Continuing along from the junction with Buzzards Roost, the trail becomes very steep, and there are actually steps cut directly into the stone landscape. This will help to get you ready for the final assault on the summit, where you will be climbing alongside and past house-sized boulders until you reach the rocky top of the mountain. A stone shelter stands on the summit, and provides shelter in inclement weather. Summer thunderstorms and lightning can at be severe on top, possibly even life threatening.

When you are ready to head down, retrace your steps in a jarring descent of the mountain back to the parking area. Unfortunately, walking along the bus road is strictly prohibited!

Total hiking distance: *3 miles round trip.*

Total hiking time: *2-3 hours.*

Elevation gain: *1,300 feet.*

Nearby attractions: Fallingwater Cascades is a lovely set of falls, and is best explored in the spring or just after a rain storm. The trailhead can be reached at mile marker 83.1 of the Blue Ridge Parkway, and is a moderate hike of 1.6 miles round trip. Flat Top Mountain is another great hike in the Peaks of Otter area, and is similar to Sharp Top Mountain with excellent views. The trailhead can be reached at mile marker 83.5 of the Blue Ridge Parkway. The hike is moderate, yet long: it is 4.5 miles one way to the top of the mountain.

Directions to trailhead: *Take Route 81 south to Roanoke, Virginia, and take exit 167 (Route 11) towards Buchanan. Follow Route 11 for 1.4 miles, and turn left on to Parkway Drive/VA 43. Go 4.7 miles and take a slight right onto the ramp for the Blue Ridge Parkway. Turn left at the Blue Ridge Parkway, and travel 4.9 miles to the Peaks of Otter.*

Sunset from Sharp Top (Ian Plant).

42

Paw Paw Tunnel
C&O Canal National Historic Park,
Maryland

Highlights: *A trip in near darkness through a half-mile historic tunnel.*

You may have noticed that manmade objects don't get a lot of mention in this book. Well, this is an exception. Located on a scenic stretch of the Chesapeake & Ohio Canal, the Paw Paw Tunnel is a rare artificial treat found in natural surroundings. Once known as one of the "Wonders of the World," now this foreboding tunnel beckons outdoor adventurers to test their will while plunging into over a half-mile of eerie darkness.

The entire length of the C&O Canal is preserved as a national park, running 185 miles from Washington, D.C. to Cumberland, Maryland. The hand-carved Paw Paw Tunnel (which is 3,118 feet long, took

12 years to build, and is made up of almost six million layered bricks), cuts through a natural feature known as the Paw Paw "bends"—an area where the Potomac River gets exceptionally wavy. Rather than build the canal following the curving river, the decision was made to go straight through the rock.

From the parking lot, follow the signs for a short hike north along the canal towpath to the tunnel. Bring a flashlight with you on this hike; it's dark inside the tunnel, and the walkway can be a bit wet and bumpy from time to time. When deep inside the tunnel, stop for a moment to admire the architecture. Then turn your

flashlight off for a while, tuning your senses to the darkness. After exiting the far end of the tunnel, hike further along the towpath through a scenic stretch of a shale-lined gorge. Take the steep, orange-blazed **Tunnel Hill Trail** back for a different perspective and great views of the Potomac River. The Tunnel Hill Trail takes you back down to the towpath, just a short distance from the parking area.

Total hiking distance: *Five miles round trip.*

Total hiking time: *1-2 hours.*

Elevation gain: *360 feet.*

Directions to trailhead: *From Winchester, Virginia, take Route 522 north for 14 miles. Turn left on to Route 127 (Bloomery Pike), eventually crossing into West Virginia. After about 10 miles, turn right on to Route 29, which after a*

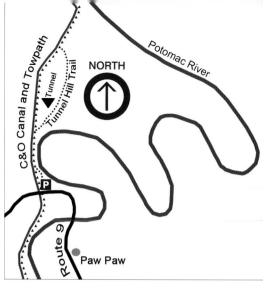

few miles becomes Route 9. Follow Route 9 through the town of Paw Paw across the Potomac River to the tunnel parking area on the right.

Inside Paw Paw Tunnel (Ian Plant).

Activities: Hiking, biking.

Access Points: Paw Paw, West Virginia.

Entrance fees: None.

Best times of year: Anytime.

43

McAfee Knob
Jefferson National Forest, Virginia

Highlights: *A strenuous hike to an Appalachian Trail icon and some of the best views in the Mid-Atlantic.*

McAfee Knob is easily one of the most famous—and photographed—spots on the Appalachian Trail. And for good reason; this is by far one of the premier spots in the greater D.C. area. Although it may lie just a tad outside of the book's three-hour driving radius from D.C., it is worth the extra time it will take to get here.

From the parking lot, cross Route 311 and start a steep ascent on the white-blazed **Appalachian Trail**. You soon reach the crest of a steep, narrow ridge taking you over rock formations. For the next few miles, you will climb up and down along the steep and rocky hillside, passing two backcountry shelters along the way (John's Spring Shelter and Catawba Mountain Shelter).

The AT continues past the second shelter and soon reaches an intersection with an old fire road. Cross the fire road for your final approach to the summit of McAfee Knob, passing several side trails that lead to views. At 3.5 miles, you will reach a signpost that says "McAfee Knob." Follow the side trail to the left and on to the Knob, which is a huge cliff with a large overhanging rock "finger" that juts out more than twenty feet. The views of the surrounding mountains are simply stupendous.

Although you will likely never want to leave, at some point you will have to head back the way you came. When you reach

Activities: Hiking, backcountry camping.

Access Points: Roanoke, Virginia.

Entrance fees: None.

Best times of year: May-October.

the intersection with the old fire road, take the road right for an easy hike back to the parking area.

There are plenty of opportunities for extended backpacking trips in the region—adventure beckons!

Total hiking distance: *7 miles round trip.*

Total hiking time: *3-4 hours.*

Elevation gain: *1,200 feet.*

Directions to trailhead: *From Route 81, take the exit for Route 419 north toward New Castle. In 0.3 miles, turn right on Route 311 north. Take Route 311 for six miles up the steep slope of Catawba Mountain. When you reach the mountain's crest, there will be a large parking area on the left for the Appalachian Trail.*

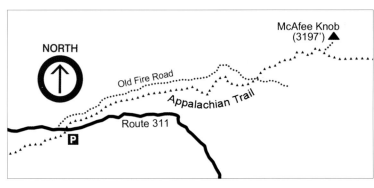

Co-author Ian Plant on the summit of McAfee Knob (self-portrait).

44

Devil's Marbleyard
Jefferson National Forest, Virginia

Highlights: *A difficult hike to a great view and an ancient crumbled cliff with boulders the size of houses.*

With a name like Devil's Marbleyard, how could your curiosity not be piqued? Such a name conjures up all kinds of diabolical visions. Despite its demonic moniker, Devil's Marbleyard is actually a very pleasant place—an amazing place, in fact!

The Marbleyard is actually the remains of an eroded cliff, a not uncommon feature for the Blue Ridge Mountains. Such old, eroded cliffs are found in a number of places throughout the region, including the summit of Old Rag Mountain, described elsewhere in this guide. What makes this one special is its size, which is significant. The Marbleyard is essentially one giant rock slide, covering much of the steep hillside.

This hike not only takes you to the Marbleyard, but also explores some of the surrounding high country for a breathtaking (both literally and figuratively) Blue Ridge loop. Shorter options are available, including just a simple jaunt to the Marbleyard and back.

Starting at the parking area, take the blue-blazed **Belfast Trail**. After a short distance, take a left on the **Glenwood Horse Trail**, which is marked with orange diamonds (the Glenwood and Belfast trails actually twist around each other and intersect twice so don't be alarmed when this happens). Keep on the Glenwood Trail for about two miles. There are a number of unmarked side trails that you will encounter; whenever you reach an intersection, just look for the orange blazes. At some point the orange blazes will disappear. Stay on the obvious wide dirt road; follow the horseshoe prints and you will be fine!

You will reach a signed intersection with the unblazed **Gunter Ridge Trail**. Turn right to begin an unrelentingly steep as-

Nearby attractions: Natural Bridge is a stunning 215-foot high natural arch. Once known as one of the "Seven Wonders of the World" and formerly owned by Thomas Jefferson, the arch is now a privately owned tourist attraction. The entrance fee is $13 for adults, $8 for children. Just make sure you visit *after* a long, sweaty hike—let the tourists know what a real adventurer smells like!

cent of Gunter Ridge. The fire-scarred ridge is fairly open with great views.

After 3.4 miles, you will reach a signed intersection. Turn right on the **Belfast Trail** toward Devil's Marbleyard. You will descend about a mile when the Marbleyard comes in on your right. You can't miss it—suddenly the trees to your right will disappear and the entire hillside will be covered with gleaming white boulders. Head out into the boulder field, and explore as much as you like.

The giant rocks at Devil's Marbleyard are 200-million year old sandstone. Look closely and you will see tiny holes in the rocks, bored by prehistoric worms when the rocks were just sandy soil. And despite their name, the rocks are not marble-like at all, but rather have rough, jagged edges.

Activities: Hiking, backcountry camping.

Access Points: Natural Bridge, Virginia.

Entrance fees: None.

Best times of year: May-October.

Be careful when scrambling up or down the boulder field. Some smaller boulders may shift as you step on them, and there are plenty of crevasses to twist an unsuspecting ankle. You will often find yourself off-balance on the boulders, so do your best to avoid falling and breaking a leg, or worse. Be on the lookout for snakes as well; copperheads and rattlesnakes may be hiding in crevasses or sunning themselves on the rocks. When you are done enjoying the Marbleyard, it is about another 1.3 miles downhill to the parking area and the end of the hike.

Total hiking distance: *8.3 miles loop.*

Total hiking time: *6-8 hours.*

Elevation gain: *1,600 feet.*

Directions to trailhead: *From Route 81, take Route 11 to Natural Bridge. Take Route 130 east toward Glasgow for three miles until you reach Natural Bridge Station. Turn right on Arnold Valley Road, and after 3 miles take a left on Petites Gap Road. The trailhead will be on the left in 1.3 miles, with a sign that says "Belfast Trail."*

The Devil's Marbleyard (Ian Plant).

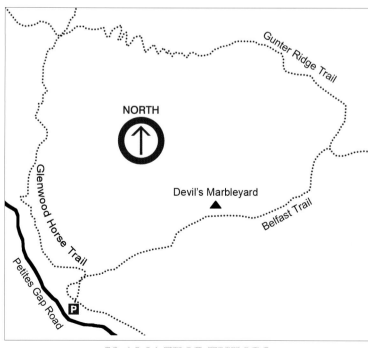

Beartown Rocks
Beartown Rocks State Park, West Virginia

Highlights: *An easy hike through a maze of moss-covered boulders and caverns.*

Beartown Rocks is a small park, only 110 acres in size, but it is a worthy place to visit nonetheless. Perched near the top of Droop Mountain, the park is known for its unusual rock formations made up of sandstone, shaped and cracked by water and ice.

The area was donated to the Nature Conservancy by a private landowner, which in turn sold the property in 1970 to the West Virginia Department of Natural Resources, which designated it a state park. The park is minimally developed in order to preserve its natural character.

The short hike described here leads you past massive boulders, overhanging cliffs, and deep crevasses. Pocketing the rocks are hundreds of eroded pits, ranging from the size of marbles to others large enough to hide within. The rocks are covered with green moss and ferns.

The name Beartown comes from a local legend that black bears once lived in the rock crevasses and caves, which have a crisscross pattern that conjures the image of city streets. Although it seems a somewhat dubious proposition, it is not hard to imagine why the legend arose—the rocks do seem an ideal place for bears!

Leaving the parking area, the path soon becomes a boardwalk that loops around

the park. Turn left or turn right, it doesn't matter: either way you will loop around and through a maze of house-sized boulders and crevasses. At the far end of the loop, a short path leads to a pleasant forest overlook.

The park is open daily from April to October. During winter when the park is closed, foot travel to the boardwalk area

Activities: Hiking.

Access Points: Hillsboro, West Virginia.

Entrance fees: None.

Best times of year: May through early October.

is welcome, with parking available before the closed entrance gate.

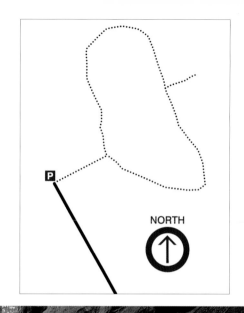

Total hiking distance: *0.5 miles loop hike.*

Total hiking time: *1 hour.*

Elevation gain: *Negligible.*

Directions to trailhead: *From Route 64, take exit 169 and turn north on Route 219. Travel 22 miles and turn right at the sign for the park. Continue a little over 1.5 miles to the parking area.*

Moss-covered rock chasm (Ian Plant).

High Falls of the Cheat
Monongahela National Forest, West Virginia

Highlights: *A hike through a beautiful forest and along a scenic railroad track to a wide, horseshoe-shaped waterfall.*

High Falls of the Cheat River is a bit of a misnomer. As it turns out, it isn't really all that high. At only twelve feet tall, it is actually a small drop compared to most of the waterfalls in this guide. But what it lacks in height it makes up for in girth. High Falls is a broad, horseshoe-shaped falls, and a spectacular sight to see in high water. And not to mention, getting there is a neat hike!

Activities: Hiking, backcountry camping.

Access Points: Glady, West Virginia.

Entrance fees: None.

Best times of year: May-October.

From the trailhead parking area, take the blue-blazed **High Falls Trail** into the forest. After crossing a foot bridge over the West Fork of the Glady River, you will pass through an open field, cross the West Fork Trail, and then begin to ascend Shavers Mountain. The trail enters the woods and ascends steeply via a series of switchbacks for about a mile, before reaching an intersection with the Allegheny Trail. Here, the forest is lush and full of ferns.

Staying on the High Falls Trail, continue past the intersection and begin a descent down into the Shavers Fork of the Cheat River valley. After another mile, the trail terminates—and here is the really neat part of the hike—at a set of railroad tracks, which run parallel to the Cheat River. Turn right (north) and follow the railroad tracks for about a half mile to High Falls. Don't worry, it is perfectly legal to walk alongside these tracks, but remember that the tracks are active (more information on that is coming), so make sure to keep off the tracks if a train is coming through the gorge.

This hike is unique because you don't actually have to hike at all to reach High Falls; you can travel in style instead. For an entirely different kind of adventure, take a ride on the Cheat Mountain Salamander

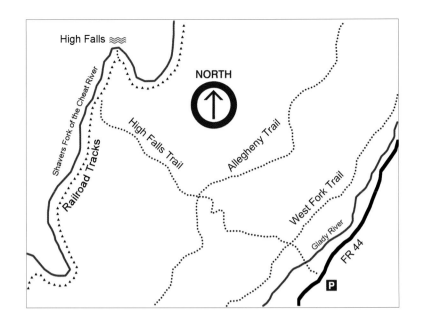

passenger train (operated by the Durbin & Greenbrier Valley Railroad) which departs from Elkins and makes a stop at High Falls!

Total hiking distance: *5 miles round trip.*

Total hiking time: *3-4 hours.*

Elevation gain: *1,400 feet (700 feet both ways).*

Directions to trailhead: *The trailhead is located off of FR 44, 4 miles south of Glady and 19 miles north of Durbin. To reach Glady, take CR 27 (Glady Road) south less than 10 miles from Route 33 (which connects Seneca Rocks and Elkins). From Glady, continue south on CR 22/2 (Beulah Road), which becomes FR 44.*

Panoramic view of High Falls of the Cheat (Ian Plant).

EPIC ADVENTURES

A kayaker in heavy waves (Ian Plant).

Appalachian Trail Traverse
George Washington National Forest, Virginia

Highlights: *A multi-day backpack along the Appalachian Trail through the area's most stunning mountain scenery.*

This epic traverse takes you 74 miles on the Appalachian Trail through the Pedlar Ranger District of the George Washington National Forest. The scenery is simply stunning, with miles and miles of wilderness, great mountain vistas, and deep forested valleys. The trail winds along and parallels the Blue Ridge Parkway all of the way, crossing the Parkway a few times before coming to Rockfish Gap at the northern terminus of the hike.

This section of the trail can be hiked either way, but is described here from north to south. Strong backpackers can probably complete the hike in as little as four days. Assuming an average of 15 miles per day, the hike can be done in five days, whereas an average of just over 10 miles per day will take seven days. Determine your strength and speed and plan accordingly, making sure to bring at least one extra day of food, just in case things take longer than expected.

There are many great views along the way, starting with Humpback Rocks in the northern end. Other superlative viewpoints include The Priest, Spy Rock, Cold Mountain, Bluff Mountain, and Fullers Rocks (overlooking the James River Gorge) shortly before you end the hike. You will also encounter countless more vistas with their own unique views.

Activities: Hiking, backcountry camping.

Access Points: Glasgow, Virginia (south); Waynesboro, Virginia (north).

Entrance fees: None.

Best times of year: May-October.

You will pass several shelters, all of which make pleasant overnight destinations: Paul C. Wolfe Shelter (mile 5.1), Maupin Field Shelter (mile 18.4), The Priest Shelter (mile 31.9), Seeley-Woodworth Shelter (mile 38.8), Cow Camp Gap Shelter (mile 48.5), Brown Mountain Creek Shelter (mile 54.1), Punchbowl Shelter (mile 62.7), and Johns Hollow Shelter (mile 71.8). In addition to the shelters, there are numerous areas suitable for tent camping. Water can sometimes be scarce on the trail, although there are stream crossings and springs at fairly regular intervals. Make sure you bring two water bottles with you, and fill them up whenever you get a chance.

Total hiking distance: *74 miles end-to-end (two car shuttle required).*

Total hiking time: *5-7 days.*

Elevation gain: *Significant and strenuous up and down climbing.*

Directions to south trailhead: *Exit Route 81 at Natural Bridge, taking Route 11 into town. Take a right at Route 130; go 6.2 miles and take a right on to Route 501. Travel 5.2 miles and take a left on to Hercules Road; travel for .9 miles to the Appalachian Trail parking area.*

Directions to north trailhead: *From Route 64, take Exit 99 for Afton Mountain. At the bottom of the exit ramp, turn right onto Route 250. In 0.2 miles, turn right on to the Skyline Drive/ Blue Ridge Parkway access road. Park at the Augusta County Visitor Center at Rockfish Gap. The Appalachian Trail is located on the east side of the Blue Ridge Parkway. Inform the visitor center staff that you will be leaving your car there for multiple nights.*

Sunset from Sky Rock along the Appalachian Trail (Ian Plant).

Bike Skyline Drive
Shenandoah National Park, Virginia

Highlights: *A multi-day bike trip along one of America's most scenic highways.*

Skyline Drive is one of the classic—and most beautiful—road bike trips in the Mid-Atlantic region. Snaking across the crest of the Blue Ridge Mountains through Shenandoah National Park, Skyline Drive runs for 105 miles from Front Royal to Waynesboro with spectacular scenery. Along the way, you will see jaw dropping vistas; interesting geological formations; and lots of wildlife. Other than hiking the length of the Appalachian Trail through the park, there is no better way of taking in the sights and sounds than to travel this scenic road on your bike.

This trip excels in another respect as well: there are plenty of lodging and dining opportunities inside the park. Thus, you can plan to take your time and enjoy the scenery, spending a night or two along the way, and not have to carry heavy bike packs full of extra equipment. You are never more than 25 miles away from

Activities: Biking.

Access Points: Front Royal and Waynesboro, Virginia.

Entrance fees: Up to $15/vehicle; varies depending on time of year.

Best times of year: May-October.

food, water, and shelter. And since the entire road is paved, this trip can be done with a road bike instead of a more cumbersome mountain bike.

Skyline Drive can be done in sections, or for the entire 105 mile length of the drive. The northernmost end of the ride begins at the Front Royal entrance station. From here, the ride begins with a steady climb for 22 miles and an elevation gain of 2,200 feet up Dickey Ridge, and finally to the Blue Ridge proper and up to Hogback Overlook at 3,385 feet. A short distance after the long climb to Hogback is a well deserved rest at Elkwallow Wayside, which has a camp store, restaurant, and restrooms. Mathews Arm campground is just 2 miles before reaching Elkwallow and is a great place to camp if you are staying overnight. Travel the rest of the northern section of the park for another seven miles, passing Jeremy's Run Overlook, Beahms Gap, and Pass Mountain Overlook, before reaching the Thornton Gap entrance station and Route 211 (which drops down to the small town of Sperryville to the east and Luray to the west). You have just covered the first section and roughly 30 miles of the length of the trip.

From Thornton Gap, you will be entering into the middle section of the park, the most diverse and breathtaking section

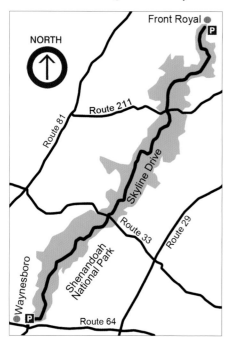

Biking along Skyline Drive (Ian Plant).

along Skyline Drive. After leaving Thornton Gap, you once again begin to climb, and not long into the ride you will pass under Mary's Rock Tunnel, the one and only tunnel along the trip. The road wanders up and down before finally reaching its highest point at Skyland, 3,680 feet. Skyland Lodge has a restaurant and great views across the Shenandoah Valley.

From here on, Hawksbill Mountain, the tallest peak in the park, dominates the view. At mile marker 46.7, you will reach Upper Hawksbill Parking Area, which is a great place to change things up a bit and hike the two mile trail to the summit. Just a little bit further down the road is Big Meadows. This is a great place to stay the night, and to do some of the hikes in the area—if you have the energy, that is! At dawn and dusk, the meadow directly across the drive from the visitor's center is filled with white-tailed deer, and in June, you may even be fortunate enough to spot a mother and her fawn. The next 15 miles of the ride will pass by some great scenic overlooks and Lewis Mountain campground. Lewis Mountain is a far more rustic and relaxed environment than the hustle and bustle of Big Meadows. From here enjoy the 1,000 foot descent from Bearfence Mountain and Lewis Mountain to Swift Run Gap.

At mile marker 65, you will reach Swift Run Gap and the last section of the trip, which takes you through the less visited southern section of the park. The scenery

Great views are around every bend of Skyline Drive (Joseph Rossbach).

is wonderful as you snake your way towards Rockfish Gap and the southern terminus of Skyline Drive. There are some really nice hikes along the way, if you have the time and energy: try walking the three miles round trip to Doyle's Falls, or, just a bit further down the road at mile marker 84.8, you can make the easy one mile loop climb to Blackrock Summit for a sunset.

When you reach Rockfish Gap, if you still feel like riding, you might consider going another 469 miles along the picturesque Blue Ridge Parkway, all the way to Great Smoky Mountains National Park in North Carolina. Of course, such a trip is outside the scope of this book just a little, but is nonetheless worth considering!

Total biking distance: *105 miles end-to-end (two car shuttle required).*

Total biking time: *Although strong riders can complete the entire length of Skyline Drive in one day, to really enjoy yourself, allow for 2-3 days of travel.*

Elevation gain: *Significant and strenuous up and down climbing.*

Directions to trailhead: *You can reach the northern section of the park from Front Royal off of Route 340. The southern terminus of Skyline Drive is reached off of Route 64 outside of Waynesboro. Parking is readily available at either end once you are inside the park past the entrance booths.*

Potomac Adventure
C&O Canal National Historic Park, Maryland

Highlights: *Bike or hike 184 miles of beautiful Potomac River scenery along this historic canal.*

For grand adventure, it doesn't get much easier than this. The Chesapeake & Ohio Canal towpath, stretching 184.5 miles from Cumberland, Maryland to Washington, D.C. is like a dirt highway for bikers and hikers. Flat and wide, it is probably the easiest way to see some of the most beautiful scenery in the greater D.C. area.

Along the way you will see many scenic attractions, some of which are described elsewhere in this book (including Great Falls and the Paw Paw Tunnel). You will be near the Potomac River almost the entire time, though you won't always be close enough to see the river. The river will change quite a bit along your journey, at times being slow and placid, and at other times fast flowing with roaring rapids and thundering waterfalls. The surrounding terrain will change as well, from low mountains around Cumberland, to the cliffs and gorges around Great Falls, to miles of flatter terrain in between.

Activities: Biking, hiking, backcountry camping.

Access Points: Cumberland, Maryland & Washington, D.C.

Entrance fees: None.

Best times of year: May through November.

The Potomac River near Carderock (Ian Plant).

This trip is best done during the spring, summer, or autumn. The height of summer can get very hot and humid, which might not make for ideal travel conditions. Travel during the spring bloom or during peak fall color can be exceptional.

Not up for the challenge of several days (by bike) or weeks (by foot) of travel? Take a smaller bite of the apple and bike or hike only a section of the canal. There are dozens of access points along the way, making it easy to custom fit a smaller journey to your tastes and abilities.

Bicycle riding is permitted only on the towpath. The surface of the towpath is hard-packed dirt trail, which can get very muddy following heavy rain. Bicyclists should be prepared to make any necessary repairs.

There are plenty of biker-hiker campsites along almost the entire length of the towpath. Finding drinkable water, even at campsites, can be a challenge. Make sure to bring along some form of water purification. As an alternative to camping, you shouldn't have much trouble finding nearby lodging and restaurants at regular intervals.

For more information about this trip, a detailed map showing camping locations, and current trail conditions, visit the National Park Service online at http://www.nps.gov/CHOH.

Total biking/hiking distance: *184.5 miles one way.*

Total biking time: *3-5 days.*

Total hiking time: *2-3 weeks.*

Elevation gain: *None.*

Directions to trailhead: *There are many access points along the Canal. The eastern terminus is in Cumberland, Maryland, whereas the western terminus is in Washington, D.C.*

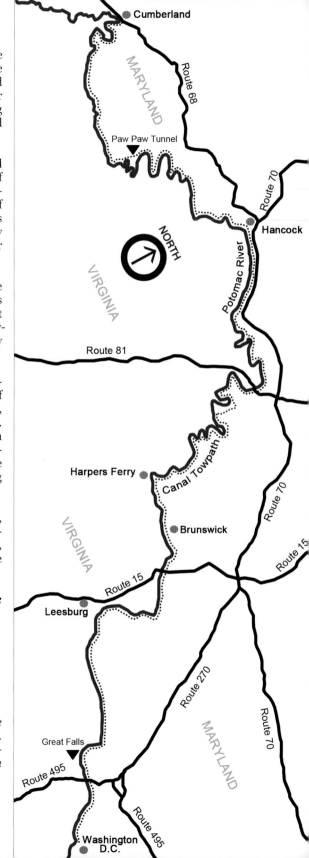

Virginia Coast Reserve
Eastern Shore of Virginia

Highlights: *A multi-day adventure for skilled kayakers though a series of wild barrier islands off the Atlantic coast.*

Activities: Sea kayaking, backcountry camping, wild adventure.

Access Points: Multiple entry points along the eastern shore of Virginia.

Entrance fees: None.

Best times of year: April-May; September-early November.

Looking to get away from it all? *Really* get away? Off the coast of Virginia lies one of the great wilderness areas of the Mid-Atlantic. It is the Virginia Coast Reserve, a string of undeveloped islands that stretch from Assateague Island to Fisherman Island on the southern tip of Cape Charles. And chances are, you'll have the whole place to yourself, making this a truly wild journey.

We don't offer any specific itinerary for this trip. It can be done from point to point, kayaking the sixty or so miles between Fisherman and Assateague Islands.

Or, you can set up a base camp and explore as you see fit. Most of the sea-side islands are owned by the Nature Conservancy, with the rest of the islands owned by either Virginia or the Federal government. Some of the islands are closed to public access at all times (Assawoman, Parramore, Little Cobb, Ship Shoal, and Fisherman). Most other islands are open for day use only (with seasonal closures in effect during bird nesting season, April 15-September 1). Primitive camping is explicitly allowed on Mockhorn Island, making it a great base for exploration. A number of the bay-side islands might make suitable overnight destinations as well. Access to the reserve is possible from a number of boat launches along the mainland.

Only those with excellent paddling and navigation skills should attempt extended exploration of the Virginia Coast Reserve. For those who are unsure of their abilities, a number of guide services offer kayak tours of the reserve, including Southeast Expeditions located in Cape Charles, Virginia (found online at www.sekayak.com).

Sunrise along the Atlantic Coast from the Virginia Coast Reserve (Ian Plant).

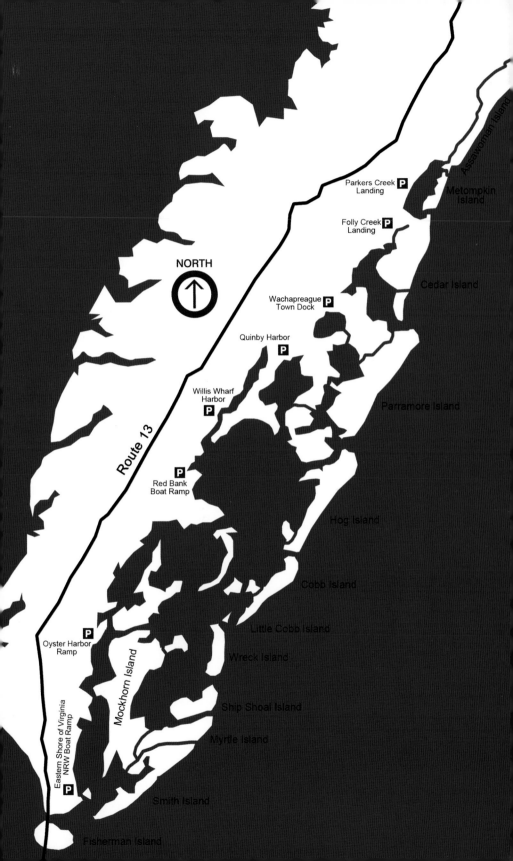

NORTH
↑

Route 13

Parkers Creek Landing **P**

Folly Creek Landing **P**

Wachapreague Town Dock **P**

Quinby Harbor **P**

Willis Wharf Harbor **P**

Red Bank Boat Ramp **P**

Oyster Harbor Ramp **P**

Eastern Shore of Virginia NRW Boat Ramp **P**

Assawoman Island

Metompkin Island

Cedar Island

Parramore Island

Hog Island

Cobb Island

Little Cobb Island

Wreck Island

Ship Shoal Island

Myrtle Island

Smith Island

Fisherman Island

Mockhorn Island

Feeding time at the Smith Island pelican colony (Ian Plant).

50 Amazing Things Checklist

		Event	Date
☐	1	Great Falls	_____
☐	2	Huntley Meadows	_____
☐	3	Ghost Fleet of the Potomac	_____
☐	4	Bull Run Spring	_____
☐	5	Kilgore Falls	_____
☐	6	Appalachian Spring	_____
☐	7	Chimney Rocks	_____
☐	8	Old Rag	_____
☐	9	Whiteoak Canyon	_____
☐	10	Whitetail Deer Fawns	_____
☐	11	Big Falls	_____
☐	12	Calvert Cliffs	_____
☐	13	Potomac Whitewater	_____
☐	14	Annapolis Rocks	_____
☐	15	A Paddle For All Seasons	_____
☐	16	Big Schloss	_____
☐	17	Cranesville Swamp	_____
☐	18	Lotus Bloom	_____
☐	19	New Point Comfort	_____
☐	20	Morris Creek	_____
☐	21	Smith Island	_____
☐	22	Janes Island	_____
☐	23	Snow Geese Explosion	_____
☐	24	Assateague Island	_____
☐	25	Big Dunes	_____
☐	26	Horseshoe Crab Spawn	_____
☐	27	Paddle with the Dolphins	_____
☐	28	A Trip Back in Time	_____
☐	29	Trough Creek Canyon	_____
☐	30	Pony Swim	_____
☐	31	Wildflowers and Rock Art	_____
☐	32	Lostland Run Loop	_____
☐	33	Swallow Falls	_____
☐	34	Blackwater Canyon	_____
☐	35	North Fork Mountain	_____
☐	36	Seneca Rocks	_____
☐	37	Bear Rocks	_____
☐	38	Rohrbraugh Plains	_____
☐	39	Crabtree Falls	_____
☐	40	Blue Ridge Traverse	_____
☐	41	Sharp Top	_____
☐	42	Paw Paw Tunnel	_____
☐	43	McAfee Knob	_____
☐	44	Devil's Marbleyard	_____
☐	45	Beartown Rocks	_____
☐	46	High Falls of the Cheat	_____
☐	47	Appalachian Trail Traverse	_____
☐	48	Bike Skyline Drive	_____
☐	49	Potomac Adventure	_____
☐	50	Virginia Coast Reserve	_____

Notes

ABOUT THE AUTHORS

Ian Plant has been photographing the natural world since 1995. His work has appeared in a number of books and calendars, as well as national and regional magazines, including *Outdoor Photographer, National Parks, Blue Ridge Country, Adirondack Life, Wonderful West Virginia,* and *Chesapeake Life,* among others. Ian is a Contributing Editor to *Nature Photographers Online Magazine.* His sixth and most recent book is the critically acclaimed "Chesapeake: Bay of Light. An Exploration of the Chesapeake Bay's Wild and Forgotten Places." Ian's work has also appeared in five books of the "Wonder and Light" series. Ian is a co-owner of **Mountain Trail Press** and **Mountain Trail Photo**, and he leads several photography workshops every year. Ian lives in Lorton, Virginia with his wife Kristin.

Joseph Rossbach has been photographing the natural world for over twelve years and has traveled to the deep canyons of the Southwest to the rugged coasts of New England in search of beautiful and evocative images of the American wilderness. Joe's work has been published in magazines, calendars, advertising campaigns, web sites, art galleries and books. A few of Joe's clients include *Blue Ridge Country, Digital Camera World, Photo Techniques Magazine, The Potomac News* and *Mountain Connections Magazine.* Joe also spends a good deal of time speaking and lecturing at regional and local camera clubs along the East Coast. Joe leads several photo tours and workshops every year through **Mountain Trail Photo.** Joe lives with his wife Amber and their son Phoenix in Annapolis, Maryland.

www.mountaintrailphoto.com

Ian and Joe are both members of the **Mountain Trail Photo** team, a collection of some of the best nature photographers in the country. The Mountain Trail Photo team is dedicated to education in the art of nature photography. The site is filled with instructional articles, equipment reviews, and location reports, along with hundreds of inspirational images from team members. There you can also find information and registration information for the team's photography workshops and tours. If you are interested in nature photography, **Mountain Trail Photo** is the site for you!